TO:

Thank You very much
for your interest in my
book, "Through Hell and High
Water."
        I hope that you will
enjoy reading it.

Leslie W. Bailey

LTC. LESLIE W. BAILEY
U.S. Army Retired
601 North Smithwick Street
Williamston, NC 27892

March 7, 1998

THROUGH HELL AND HIGH WATER

*The Wartime Memories of a
Junior Combat Infantry Officer*

**Lieutenant Colonel Leslie W. Bailey,
United States Army (Retired)**

VANTAGE PRESS
New York

FIRST EDITION

Copyright © 1994 by Lieutenant Colonel Leslie W. Bailey,
United States Army (Retired)

Published by Vantage Press, Inc.
516 West 34th Street, New York, New York 10001

Manufactured in the United States of America
ISBN: 0-533-10942-6

Library of Congress Catalog Card No.: 93-95057

0 9 8 7 6 5 4 3 2 1

Affectionately dedicated to my late wife, Sarah, at whose suggestion this book was written and who waited patiently at home in Williamston, North Carolina, throughout the long, bitter months during which the action described in this book transpired

Contents

Foreword   vii

Acknowledgments   ix

    I. New Arrival at Fort Dix, New Jersey   1

   II. Staging Area   6

  III. The Voyage to Ireland   10

  IV. Ballycastle   14

   V. Sojourn in Omagh   18

  VI. Exercise Atlantic   22

 VII. Inveraray, Scotland   26

VIII. Final Training for a Top Secret Voyage   30

  IX. Invasion!   34

   X. Palace Guards   57

  XI. Preparation for Combat   65

 XII. Journey to Tunisia   70

XIII. On the Defensive in Pichon   74

XIV. Retreat from Pichon   79

 XV. Routine Patrol Activity   84

XVI. The Battle of Fondouk Pass   88

XVII. Rehearsal for the Next Battle   99

XVIII. The Battle of Hill 609   104

XIX. Victory at Last—in North Africa   112

 XX. Siesta Period   117

XXI. School Days Again—in North Africa   121

XXII. Company Commander   126

XXIII. Sunny Italy   129

XXIV. The First Crossing of the Volturno   131

XXV. The Second Crossing of the Volturno   137

XXVI. The Third Crossing of the Volturno   142

XXVII. Mountains, Rain, and Mud   144
XXVIII. Respite from Battle   154
XXIX. Anzio   162
XXX. Pursuit   173
XXXI. Rotation   178

Epilogue   181
Appendices
    Appendix A. Field Order for Attack of Third Battalion,
        135th Infantry, on Harbor of Algiers, North Africa, on
        Morning of 8 November 1942   185
    Appendix B. Field Order for Attack of Company K
        (Reinforced), 135th Infantry (Malcolm Group), on
        Harbor of Algiers, North Africa, on Morning of 8
        November 1942   188
    Appendix C. Maps of Landing Operations in North Africa
        on November 8, 1942   190
Index   195

Foreword

When I look back in retrospect at my combat experiences in World War II, the quotations of two great Americans, Benjamin Franklin and Gen. William T. Sherman, immediately come to mind. Dr. Franklin once said, "There never was a good war or a bad peace." General Sherman expressed his feelings on war even more bluntly with the words, "War is Hell."

I agree with both of these quotations. However, anyone familiar with ancient and modern history must surely realize that even though all wars are bad, a nation is sometimes forced into a war following an attack upon its territory by an aggressor nation or group of nations. World War II was this kind of war for the United States and many of its allies.

During World War II, I served in combat in the U.S. Army Thirty-fourth Infantry Division in North Africa and Italy as an infantry platoon leader, rifle company commander, and infantry battalion executive officer.

Shortly after I returned on rotation to the United States in September 1944, at the suggestion of my wife, Sarah, I started writing a narrative account of my wartime experiences at Fort Dix, New Jersey; in Northern Ireland; and in North Africa and Italy. I completed writing the first draft of my manuscript in 1945.

After numerous revisions extending over more than forty-eight years my manuscript is finally being published under the title *Through Hell and High Water.*

I am well aware of the fact that a multitude of books about World War II have already been published by great heroes of the war such as Audie Murphy, *To Hell and Back*; by great war correspondents such as Ernie Pyle, *Here Is Your War* and *Brave Men*; and by famous generals such as Omar N. Bradley, *A Soldier's Story,* and George S. Patton, Jr., *War as I Knew It.*

Despite this fact, for many years I have steadfastly believed that there is an urgent need for one more book about World War II—a book that presents a unique and dramatically realistic account of what life was like in the infantry for ordinary young officers and enlisted men in North Africa and Italy.

My book, *Through Hell and High Water*, fulfills this urgent need. Instead of relating the valiant deeds of a few great heroes or the glorious victories of the war's greatest generals, it offers a simple, factual, unembellished worm's-eye view of the war as seen through the eyes of an often scared young infantry officer. It tells the candid story of the desperate fears, frustrations, and bitter hardships suffered by this typical, foot-slogging, young infantry officer and his men as they stoically endured the trials and tribulations of endless days and nights of engaging in a series of small unit actions against a ruthless enemy in North Africa and Italy. Moreover, it also emphasizes with stark clarity my most unforgettable wartime memories; fear, confusion, cold, mud, darkness, suffering, and death of both friend and foe. At the same time *Through Hell and High Water* closely relates my observations and experiences to the great events and to the great actors who performed in the center of the stage of World War II history.

Acknowledgments

I wish to express my appreciation to my West Point classmate (USMA 1941), U.S. Army Col. Horace M. Brown (Ret.) of Weaverville, N.C., a fellow World War II veteran of combat service in Italy, for his valuable suggestions for publicizing and marketing this book. Also, I wish to express my special thanks to my daughter, Mrs. Rosanne B. Mitchell, of 14010 Minnehaha Place, Wayzata, Minnesota, for carefully reading and reviewing it, and for making many constructive comments concerning its content and literary style. Likewise, I wish to thank Mrs. Vickie Carr of Williamston, N.C., for her hard work, patience, and skill in typing the draft of my book in a final form fit for editing prior to its publication. Finally, I wish to thank Camille Hyder of the Vantage Press editorial staff for the professional skill which she clearly demonstrated by using her exceptional knowledge of history and English grammar and composition so effectively in completing the tedious task of editing the final draft of my manuscript.

Chapter I

New Arrival at Fort Dix, New Jersey

At Fort Dix, New Jersey, on 9 February 1942, the snow swirled in feathery flakes from the lead gray clouds that chased each other across a winter sky. As I walked toward the low frame building of the U.S. Army, Thirty-fourth Infantry Division Headquarters, a gust of icy wind suddenly lifted my hat from my head and set it down violently in the grimy snow on the ground just ahead of me.

As a second lieutenant, newly arrived from Fort Bragg, North Carolina, I was anxious to create a good impression on my military superiors at Fort Dix, but the mud, snow, and cold were deepening my anxiety and dampening my enthusiasm.

As soon as the customary formality of signing my name, date of arrival, and authority for assignment to the Thirty-fourth Division was completed, its adjutant general informed me that I must start at once to get my personal affairs in order for a long boat trip to an undisclosed destination.

Next I was instructed to report to Capt. Robert V. Shinn, the 135th Infantry regimental adjutant, for further assignment. After a few words of welcome from Captain Shinn, I reported to Capt. Arthur A. Kanstrup, commanding officer of Company H, 135th Infantry. Upon my arrival at the Company H Headquarters, Captain Kanstrup asked if I knew anything about 81-mm mortars. I told him the only 81-mm mortars I had ever seen were the wooden ones we used on the Carolina maneuvers.

"Well, I see you have grasped the basic facts about mortars." He smiled. "You have got yourself a job. You will be the platoon leader of the Eighty-one-Millimeter Mortar Platoon of the Second Battalion, 135th Infantry Regiment. There are four squads of soldiers and four mortars in your platoon. Sergeant Thompson is your platoon sergeant. Report to me at 0600 hours tomorrow for duty. Meanwhile, move your trunk and personal belongings into your quarters, meet your noncommissioned officers, and look over the immediate area and quarters of your men. Your quarters will be in the large end room in barracks number three, on the second floor with First Lieutenants Muir and Nelson. The other two officers in the company are Second Lieutenants Walsh and Siats."

Since it was late in the afternoon, it was dark before I finished moving my footlocker, uniforms, and other personal equipment into my quarters, which were in wooden barracks, two stories in height, and long and low in silhouette. The men of the 135th Infantry lived in rows of these buildings, with each of the three battalions of approximately eight hundred men surrounding a large central quadrangle, which was used for close-order drill and other formations of the regiment. Each company had its own mess hall in which the men received three delicious and nutritious meals daily.

The officers and enlisted men of my new company were a sturdy, industrious group. Most of them were from Minnesota and were of Swedish or Norwegian ancestry. They had lived a rugged outdoor life before their induction a year before as a National Guard company called into federal service. Now with more than a year of intensive military training in the rainy swamplands of Camp Claiborne, Louisiana, behind them they were well suited either to endure the rigors of further cold weather at Fort Dix or go immediately overseas and fight the Germans.

Our training day at Fort Dix was long and gruelling. Our motto was: A Busy Man Is a Happy Man, and we lived up to it. Out of bed long before daylight, officers and men were required to stand reveille formation at 0600 hours. Proper uniform consisted of heavy woolen underwear, woolen trousers and blouse, woolen gloves, woolen caps, shoes, heavy woolen overcoat, canvas leggings, and a necktie. Breakfast at 0650 was followed by a busy morning training schedule, which lasted from 0750 until 1200 and consisted of close-order drill; infantry tactics; and the operation, manipulation, and firing of infantry weapons, such as mortars, machine guns, and rifles. Our afternoon schedule usually included a march of from eight to twelve miles with full field packs and rifles through the wooded hills and brush country that surround Fort Dix and from which we seldom returned before 1600 hours. This gave us thirty minutes to wash away the sweaty grime and dress in our best uniforms for the retreat formation at 1650 hours. Following retreat, we had a period of rest until supper at 1750 hours. From 1850 until 1950 all officers and NCOs were required to attend a one-hour period of critique and orientation for the next day's work. After the critique, held daily except Saturdays and Sundays, it was necessary for those who wanted to leave the post to get dressed in their best uniforms. Because of our alert status, only 15 percent of the enlisted men were permitted to leave the post each day.

Officers were also stringently restricted. An officer was required to get permission from both his company commander and battalion commander in order to leave the post. All second lieutenants and first lieutenants were called junior officers and were required to behave in a respectful manner to officers of higher rank.

One second lieutenant soon found out that discipline at Fort Dix was prompt and severe. He made a trip to Trenton, New Jersey, without permission of his company commander and was spotted by a first lieutenant who reported him, with the result that the second lieutenant was restricted to quarters for a period of one week. I was careful in avoiding such pitfalls. As a result I got along fine and within one month was wearing the shiny silver bars of a first lieutenant.

The most difficult part of our service at Fort Dix was caused by the actions of a senior regular army general officer, who apparently had the opinion that the 135th Infantry was below minimum requirements for entering combat. He seemed determined not only

3

that we should immediately correct our faults, but that we could not do so without his firm guidance.

Thereafter, he conducted what seemed to be a continuous motorized patrol whose objective was to inculcate each of us as quickly as possible with the basic attributes of a soldier. It was soon evident that one of the greatest sins of a military man was to be seen with his hands in his pockets and to fail to respond with sufficient alacrity to his resonant bellow, "Take your hands out of your pockets!"

The situation reached its climax one Sunday morning at about 0800 hours when the general arrived with the suddenness and surprise of the Japanese planes attacking Pearl Harbor and proceeded to make an inspection of the officers' quarters. Most of the officers were away for the weekend. The only one present was a major, taking a nap on the top of his bed. When the general saw that some of the beds were not made, his eyes continued to scan the room until they rested on the reclining form of the major. The general immediately ordered the major to his feet and threatened to relieve him from command for inefficiency and neglect of duty. The order was immediately dispatched by telegraph and telephone to all officers of the 135th Infantry to return at once to their quarters, and those present were instructed to make all beds and thoroughly scrub the barracks for a rigorous, formal inspection to be held at 1400 hours that same day.

Only seven officers were available to clean the barracks. Consequently, we spent the rest of the morning and most of the afternoon in the disagreeable task of making beds and scrubbing floors. Meanwhile, my wife, Sarah, at my urgent request, rushed from our apartment in the nearby town of Mount Holly to assist me in cleaning the barracks.

Suddenly, someone yelled in a frightened voice, "Look out, here he comes! Attention!"

Evidently Sarah, my wife of only four weeks, had an unfortunate first impression of the U.S. Army. Reacting as though the devil himself was in the immediate vicinity, she, without a backward glance, sped like a frightened deer through the door at the opposite end of the barracks from the one through which the inspecting officer had just entered. She moved so fast he never saw her. However, the alarm was unnecessary, as the inspecting officer turned out to be a kind-hearted brigadier general who made the inspection without incident and afterwards stated that everything appeared to be in fine shape.

After the inspection we were ordered to move our bedding and equipment to a building about two miles away, from which we had to march each morning in military formation in groups, under the command of the senior-ranking lieutenant colonel of each battalion, to our old area to stand reveille at 0600 hours with our troops. We were first required to bounce out of our beds each morning at 0450 hours, dress fully, stand an officers' reveille formation, then afterwards wash, shave, and fall out promptly for our morning march to our respective company areas.

Chapter II
Staging Area

Life in our staging area at Fort Dix passed quickly and quietly after these incidents. Several lieutenants got married, but the imminence of our overseas journey loomed so great that such weddings had to be accomplished on weekends and any possibility of taking a honeymoon postponed until the end of the war.

Rumors abounded throughout our stay at Fort Dix. But due to increased German submarine activity at this time, our sailing was delayed successively from February to March to April.

The question with which every wife in the regiment greeted her husband at the end of each day was, "When are you going to sail?" Few seemed to realize that the urgency of the military situation required such information to be kept secret and that even if we knew, we could not tell our wives. On 28 April we were placed on a twenty-four-hour alert, with all telephone and telegraph communication prohibited with all those not on the post. Most of us saw our wives and families for the last time at midnight on 28 April 1942. After that, no civilian was allowed to enter Fort Dix. However, several of the officers' wives, including Sarah, sneaked into their husbands' small rooms in the barracks just before midnight and managed to spend a last night with them without being discovered. Consequently, they had to arise before dawn on 29 April and sneak silently away and off the post, with their last good-byes whispered quietly and sadly in the darkness.

At last, during the afternoon of 29 April, we loaded on a long convoy of two-and-half-ton trucks and started the short journey to the Fort Dix railway station. As the motors roared into life, I glanced at my watch and noted the time was 1650 hours.

No doubt each of the three thousand men who climbed aboard the trucks that afternoon was saddened that secrecy had prevented his family from seeing him off, but as far as I know, only one man balked at the last minute. As he struggled to lift his heavy barracks bag over the tailgate of the truck, he burst into tears and turned to run. A burly sergeant grabbed him by the shoulders and, despite his tears and protests, threw him heavily aboard the truck.

After only a few minutes of travel, we arrived at the Fort Dix railway station to find an empty passenger train already drawn up on the tracks to receive us. The debarkation from the trucks and into the train was smooth, swift, and orderly. Without a hitch, we filed slowly into the train, settled wearily into our seats, and glumly glanced outside at the empty station where no one was present to bid us good-bye. However, we had but little time to feel sorry for ourselves. Our train started with a sudden jolt and began to roll slowly toward New York City.

As I sat silently staring out the left window beside my seat, we passed through several deserted street crossings where the gate bars were down and the signal bells were clanging loudly and raucously. Suddenly I espied a single blue, 1941 model Chevrolet automobile at the last street-crossing site, facing the path of our train. Suddenly, too late for me to wave or yell good-bye, I clearly saw and instantly realized that the lone car facing the railroad trucks was *my car* and that its sole occupant was my wife, Sarah, sitting forlornly behind its steering wheel.

With desperate tenacity and uncommon perspicacity, she had entered Fort Dix on a seldom-used road through an unguarded rear entrance of the post. Subsequently, she had skillfully managed to outwit and elude the vigilant military police guards on the post until she was able to approach close enough to an unguarded railroad crossing through which she hoped our troop train would travel. She did all this so she could get one last glimpse of us as we travelled

7

swiftly into a future of uncertainty, war, and possible death. However, our train passed through the crossing so quickly, she did not see me. But the sad, dejected image of Sarah, sitting alone in our car on an empty street at a deserted railroad crossing at Fort Dix, New Jersey, on 29 April 1942, is one I shall never forget.

As the steam locomotive pulling our train gradually gained momentum and puffed swiftly through the green countryside of rural New Jersey, the shadows of evening slowly lengthened and the sun soon sank from view behind the rose-tinted clouds in the west. As twilight deepened and the last sunbeams faded from the sky, we sadly realized that it would be many months before we would again see the bright sunshine of the U.S.A.

It seemed but a few minutes before our arrival at the New York port of embarkation, where our train stopped. We dismounted immediately and moved on foot aboard a small ferry boat, which crossed a dark body of water and deposited us on a huge dock beside a large ship, which, presumably, we would soon board. Meanwhile, the moon had risen and shed its brilliant light over the dark waters of the harbor. A low murmur of conversation rose from the men and soon mingled with the medley of noises and eerie sounds that filled New York Harbor.

We were able for the first time to see the large four-stack British ship, *Aquitania*. She was a welcome sight because of the persistent rumor that we would ride a dirty cattle boat to Europe.

Although eager to go aboard, we were forced to wait almost two hours in a long, sweating, cursing, milling line of frustrated infantrymen, which inched forward so slowly it seemed not to move at all. Each enlisted man was loaded with a fifty-pound pack, an M-1 rifle, and two large laundry bags, crammed almost to bursting with blankets, clothes, shoes, and miscellaneous articles, all of which he desperately struggled to balance on his shoulders. Each time the line began to move, the men would grab their heavy burdens in eager anticipation and start forward only to set them down with frustrated curses of rage a few seconds later as all forward movement of the line ceased.

We were lined up in a previously typed passenger-list order, and as the surname of each man was called, he answered in a loud voice with his first name and middle initial. It was well past 2200 hours when the last man finally clambered wearily up the gangplank into the ship.

Chapter III
The Voyage to Ireland

The first duty of a good leader on boarding an army transport is to go belowdecks immediately and see that his men are comfortably quartered. In my attempt to carry out this duty, I wandered belowdecks for several minutes before I located the men of my platoon. I finally found them with the remainder of Company H, on E deck, the fifth down from the top deck, in the left stern of the ship.

The quarters seemed to be fairly comfortable. Each man was assigned a folding canvas cot with an iron frame. These cots were in tiers of four and fastened to vertical metal pipes. There were no mattresses, but each man was allowed two blankets. The most serious fault of their location was the constant noise of the ship's propeller, which made it difficult for men to sleep until their ears became accustomed to the noise.

Since army transport regulations require that a ship compartment occupied by enlisted men must have an officer present in it twenty-four hours a day, I expected to spend a lot of time with my men, particularly since there were only three officers in H Company available for this duty.

After making the required initial check of the quarters of my platoon, I proceeded up to the A deck and found that as an officer I rated first-class accommodations in a large stateroom with five other officers, including the regimental chaplain and dentist.

The daily routine of military personnel aboard ship was mild indeed compared to the vigorous life we had led at Fort Dix. The only required military formations were reveille at 0600 hours, a one-hour period of calisthenics at 0850 hours, and a lifeboat drill at 1000 hours.

The object of the lifeboat drill was to ensure that each of the approximately seven thousand men would know in advance the exact location of his lifeboat or life raft and the correct path to follow to reach it in case of sudden disaster. In case of an air raid, all troops were required to go belowdecks and stay until the sounding of the all clear signal.

During daylight hours, everyone stayed on deck to enjoy the warm sunshine, blue skies, and gentle breezes of the Gulf Stream. During hours of darkness, a strict blackout was enforced, with no smoking permitted on the weather decks between sunset and sunrise.

Although a strict twenty-four hour alert was maintained, no enemy ships, planes, or submarines were sighted. The battleships, aircraft carriers, and destroyers that accompanied us were responsible for our being one of the largest convoys that had ever before crossed the Atlantic Ocean.

Throughout the trip the spirits of officers and men were high, partly because of the wonderful weather and partly because of the presence of our regimental band, The Ambassadors of Swing, which enlivened each afternoon by a rendition of the men's favorite songs, such as "The Old Gray Mare" and "There's a Man Comes to Our House Every Single Day." The morale of the officers received an additional boost by having the grand ballroom of the *Aquitania*, with its rich furnishings and beautiful paintings, set aside as their recreation room and bar.

The enlisted men were provided with adequate recreational facilities in a large room belowdecks. Some of the men were soon busy playing cards and shooting dice. Others carried with them a wealth of magazines, pocket books, and detective stories, which they read then exchanged with their comrades. Additionally, the welcome rum ration received each day from the British navy boosted their morale almost higher than the daily fare of Australian mutton lowered it. (We had lamb daily on our menu because the *Aquitania* had just taken on a cargo of meat during her recent visit to Australia.) The British custom of halting all activity promptly each day at 1650 hours for a refreshing "cup o' tea" won the approval of everyone.

Our course led us past Halifax, Nova Scotia, at the mouth of the Saint Lawrence River, where we paused to await the arrival of several ships scheduled to join our convoy. The land was a welcome sight, but no one was permitted to go ashore.

Much of the time of the junior officers was spent in censoring letters written by the enlisted men. Every letter had to be read by an officer and any references to the name of our ship, its destination, armament, food, quarters, or sailing date had to be deleted either by clipping or requiring the letter to be rewritten. These restrictions reduced the subject matter of the letters but not their quantity. Although they could not be mailed until our arrival in Ireland, the enlisted men continued to write many letters.

Our voyage was without excitement except for one incident, which occurred as we were sitting down to noon chow on the fourth day out from New York. A series of four terrific explosions suddenly shattered the stillness. My first reaction was that we were being attacked by the entire German navy and air force. As I attempted to dash on deck to discover the trouble, I collided with terrific force against a panic-stricken enlisted man, who was using the same route as I but in the opposite direction. Both of us rolled in an ignominious heap to the bottom of the stairs. When I arrived on deck, minus my life preserver, which, in violation of orders, I had forgotten to carry, I found that the explosions had been caused by a destroyer, which had dropped a few depth bombs in the direction in which its radar had indicated a German submarine. Shamefacedly, I returned to my unfinished meal.

On the following day, the ship's newspaper published an official German radio announcement that the "British troopship, *Aquitania*, had just been destroyed by a German submarine, with the loss of all on board." On the same day we received the gloomy news of the fall of Corregidor and the surrender of General Wainwright and his men in the Philippine Islands.

Just before dusk on 14 May 1942, we first sighted land to our starboard. Preparations were started immediately to get ready to debark on the following morning.

Chapter IV
Ballycastle

The next morning we rose long before daylight, breakfasted, cleaned the ship thoroughly of all debris and refuse, and debarked on a small ship that was barely large enough to hold the troops of our Second Battalion. For several hours our little vessel moved slowly in total darkness across the smooth surface of a large body of water.

When the sun finally appeared in the azure sky, the beautiful vista made me think of the Emerald City in the Land of Oz. The glistening white houses contrasted sharply against the emerald of the gently rolling hills covered with fields separated by well-kept hedges extending to the water's edge. I saw only a few scattered trees anywhere on the landscape.

It was almost noon before we arrived at the large Ulster city of Londonderry. Only a few British officers and one American officer were present to greet us officially. Among the small crowd of onlookers were two trim Army Territorial Service (A.T.S.) sergeants, the first female soldiers we had ever seen.

Following our smoothly efficient debarkation, we ate a refreshing meal of hot coffee, bread, potatoes, and luncheon meat.

Little time was allowed for sightseeing. Instead, we boarded large trucks called lorries, which took up intervals of a hundred yards between them to avoid presenting a tempting target to any German bombers that might have received word of our arrival in Northern Ireland.

As we rode through the streets of Londonderry, I noticed that its buildings were like those of a city of similar size in the United States. However, the lack of motor vehicles was a sharp contrast to urban traffic conditions in the U.S.A. I saw only a few U.S. Army trucks, British lorries, and small private cars on the streets of the city.

As our convoy moved slowly along the winding road, which passed through the Irish countryside, I noticed other contrasts. There were few trees and no forests. All houses were of white stone with tile or slate roofs. Everything seemed on a smaller scale than in the U.S.A. Both fields and houses were smaller, with a farmhouse usually serving as a barn for the farm animals as well as a dwelling for the farmer and his family.

The roads of Northern Ireland were not built to accommodate the high speeds of modern automobiles. They were so narrow and circuitous that high speed on them was difficult to achieve. Consequently, it was late in the afternoon before we reached our destination, the village of Ballycastle, on the extreme northern tip of Northern Ireland.

We unloaded quickly and, with the help of a smooth-working committee of British army officers, were soon able to install the eight hundred men of our battalion in a number of private homes, scattered to prevent high casualties in the event of German air raids.

Life at Ballycastle settled into a pleasant routine. We soon made many friends among the people. Since we were the first American troops to enter the town, there were no prejudices against us. Because so many of us were of Scotch-Irish ancestry it seemed we were among our own people. It was often difficult to understand their dialect but we had no difficulty in understanding their warmhearted hospitality. We were frequently guests in their homes. As a result of these visits, such terms as *Chemist's Shop* for drug store, *Iron Mongery* for hardware store and *hairdresser* for barber shop were soon added to our vocabulary.

During the first two days of our sojourn at Ballycastle the weather was fair and mild, which gave us the chance to look about us. The town was situated on the grass-covered slopes of a small plateau that dropped off in a sheer cliff of several hundred feet straight down to the edge of a sapphire sea. The brilliant sunshine and the churning white foam of the waves lapping against the rocks at the base of the cliff looked inviting, but the water was still too cold for us to swim in it.

After two days the beautiful weather came to an abrupt end. Thereafter the sky was continuously overcast with slate-colored clouds from which rain fell every day for four-and-one-half months. A chilling wind blew shoreward from the sea, necessitating the wearing of warm woolen clothing.

Although we made many hikes through the peat bogs on the hills and in the heather-strewn valleys, we dared not leave shelter for more than ten minutes without raincoats. The rain usually didn't last long but intermittently for so long that the moisture in the air prevented wet clothing from drying.

The typical Irish summer day was ushered in by sunrise at 7:00 A.M. However we seldom saw the sun because of the thick blanket of gray clouds covering the sky. Usually at around 9:00 A.M. these clouds cleared away, permitting fleeting glimpses of the sun and sky. Then the clouds thickened and a steady downpour of rain fell for several minutes. Normally this continued for only a few minutes and then the unending cycle of clouds and sun, clouds and rain continued. The bad weather caused me to catch a severe chronic cold from which I never recovered until I left Ireland.

Twilight came late and lingered long during the Irish summer. Sunset occurred at about 11:30 P.M. so that it was usually 1:00 A.M. before the inky blackness of the Irish night arrived. I cannot remember having seen the moon or the stars because of the clouds. The Irish people have often been accused of being heavy whiskey drinkers, but I think anyone who has spent any time at all in the dreary, drab climate of Northern Ireland will admit that a strong brand of whiskey might be necessary for the natives to relieve the monotony of such a climate.

Their favorite beverage was Old Bushmills Irish Whiskey, which retailed for ten dollars per quart and had a kick comparable to Kikapoo Joy Juice. Their beer was called stout, or Guinness. Al Jolson, during his visit to Northern Ireland in the summer of 1942, remarked that as far as he was concerned they might as well pour the Irish beer back into the horses.

After sundown a rigid blackout was enforced in all parts of Northern Ireland. Bars were required to close at 7:00 P.M., but this rule was often ignored. Some of the bars remained open on a speakeasy basis until past midnight, during which time dancing, gambling, and drinking were freely indulged in by all those present.

The prevailing religion was Protestant, with five such churches located in Ballycastle. With the arrival of the first Sunday our entire battalion attended the Presbyterian Church and listened to a sermon by Chaplain Bell on the subject "The Fighting Battalion," during which he reminded us that we were here to *fight* and not to enjoy pleasant surroundings and that many of us would soon be resting in eternal sleep beneath the grassy sod.

The chaplain's words seemed like undue pessimism but later events proved them to be prophetic, since he himself was destined to die bravely in action in the battle of Fondouk, North Africa, while on a mission of mercy to move from a German minefield the dead bodies of many of those who sat in his congregation on that bright Sunday morning in May 1942.

After the sermon the local mayor made a speech and said the Irish people could never repay us for coming to liberate them and that they would be indebted to us forever.

We stayed in Ballycastle for only two weeks, during which time our training consisted mainly of long hikes. Shortly after dawn on 1 June 1942, we once more climbed aboard our trucks and headed in a southeasterly direction toward the large town of Omagh in County Tyrone, near the border of the Irish Free State.

Chapter V
Sojourn in Omagh

The road to Omagh was hard-surfaced, but like many other Irish roads, it was narrow and crooked. Most of the population was lined along both sides of the road to honor us on the occasion of our departure. The children of the villages along our route screamed wildly and made the V sign with both hands as we passed. Pretty Irish colleens (young girls) along the way showered our slow-moving jeeps with a constant stream of roses and bouquets of wild flowers. Under this undeserved adulation for still unproven valor, the chests of many a second lieutenant stuck out like that of a conquering Caesar making his triumphal entry into Rome after a victorious struggle against the barbarians.

At the end of the first day's travel, we bivouacked for two days at the edge of a large forest on the estate of a member of the Irish landed gentry. The ivy-covered stone castle where the battalion officers were billeted was surrounded by a wide lawn in the center of which stood a big circular sundial. Emerging from the dense forest of moss-covered oak and beech trees at the right front of the house, a gurgling stream flowed from an artificial lake and leaped down for fifty feet into a foamy whirlpool at the base of a waterfall that was shaded by the branches of four stately copper beech trees.

Near the castle, which was owned by a lady member of the British Parliament, stood several Quonset huts built under the shade of beech trees to hide them from German reconnaissance planes. In these there was sufficient room for all the men of our battalion. The huts were typical of those scattered throughout the British Isles and represented the contribution of the large landowners of Britain toward the winning of the war.

Early on the third day of our stay at this delightful retreat we boarded our trucks and resumed our journey toward Omagh, a town of approximately five thousand inhabitants.

After four hours of slow travel, we arrived in the narrow streets of the town to find a large crowd lined along the street to greet us. Two conspicuous members of this informal greeting committee were soon noted leaning far out of a second-story window. One was a beautiful curvaceous brunette in a bulging red sweater and the other one was a honey-haired blonde with an equal amount of beauty and streamlining in a blue sweater. Both smiled and waved and yelled with such fervor as to elicit whistles and shouts of approval from the lips of eight hundred officers and men of our battalion.

These distracting influences did not long delay us since we were anxious to get settled quickly in our new homes, which an advance billeting party of officers had already prepared for us. Most of the battalion was quartered in Quonset huts spread under trees throughout the town, but the officers and men of Company H were led into the dark, damp corridors of an old rambling stone building that had formerly been the County Poorhouse for the Aged.

Our new home stood on a grassy hill among a grove of oak and elm trees, which further restricted the sunlight from entering the gloomy stone walls of the poorhouse. It was surrounded by a high cement wall and was divided into two courtyards on the inside, one of which we used as a motor pool for parking the twenty-four motor vehicles of the battalion and the other as the area for Company H to stand the daily reveille and retreat formations. The front of the poorhouse opened into the streets of Omagh. Behind it was a small peat bog and some higher hills covered with fields of Irish potatoes and bisected at regular intervals by high hedges extending in several directions.

The rooms of the poorhouse were so filthy it took several hours of thorough cleaning with brooms, mops, G.I. soap, and elbow grease before they were ready for human occupancy, but even the thorough cleaning of the gloomy building failed to dispel the depressing atmosphere of a prison.

However, there was no time for self-pity. We had much work to do in starting a training program to teach men to fight as squad and platoon teams in the larger Company H team. My task was to train each of the four eight-man eighty-one-millimeter mortar squads in my platoon to act together as a strong platoon team that would be able in combat to lay down a coordinated barrage of shells into the ranks of the enemy. I hoped that this training would permit us to be the most powerful force in the battalion in knocking out enemy machine guns and mortars that might later oppose our advance. We were trained to fire mortars from positions eight hundred yards behind our assaulting infantry rifle troops and to launch high explosive shells with deadly accuracy at targets up to 3,280 yards away. In addition to attaining technical proficiency with our individual and team weapons, we were always faced with the problem of keeping the men physically hardened by long hikes and calisthenics, and having them run over obstacle courses, which included high stone walls, deep pits, and trenches. It was necessary to maintain strict discipline and to indoctrinate the men with the aggressive will to close with and destroy the enemy at close range on his own ground.

Besides the rigorous training there were many hours of leisure for officers and men. These were replete with dances, afternoon teas, picnics, bicycle rides, and sightseeing tours into the country.

At one of the officers' parties, which was attended by many local ladies, the beautiful brunette, Ulster's Queen of Song, who had worn the red sweater on the day of our arrival, accompanied by our Ambassadors of Swing sang "Danny Boy" and "The White Cliffs of Dover." During a break between songs, a young lieutenant from Georgia was engaged in an animated conversation with her until someone whispered in her ear that she could make a big hit

ng our return from maneuvers on 10 July, we spent or
esting and cleaning our rusty weapons, muddy equi
othing. During this period so many letters were writte
hat the officers of Company H had to set up a syste
g clerical and administrative assistants to help them
e mail. The man who wrote the most letters in any or
esignated by his platoon leader as the clerical ar
e assistant of the platoon during his leisure time f
g week. The number of letters that the enlisted m
iately dropped off.

the second week after our maneuvers, we increas
our daily hikes from fifteen to twenty. On one of the
ted for lunch on the palatial wooded estate of the du
, the governor general of Northern Ireland. The esta
idreds of acres of oak, beech, and birch trees, whi
he largest forest in Northern Ireland, and, of course
autiful mansion.

vernor general's teenage grandson and granddaught
fficers of Company H into their mansion and conduct
of the interior, showing us many relics that dated ba
years.

jects that provided the greatest interest to me were t
eenhouses in the governor's gardens in which grew,
ich fruits as peaches, pears, and tomatoes.

the last half of July and the first half of August, ea
the regiment was required to spend a week at each
g centers established by Lieutenant Colonel Drake, o
ns and training officer, to simulate actual combat.
the training was thorough, with part of a battalion us
enemy and the rest as attacking infantrymen support
which fired live ammunition over our heads. Hik
idrawals, defense, and night operations were contin
time for rest. We had rain, as usual, day and night
k at one of these training centers. The knee-deep m

with him by singing his favorite song, "Marching through Georgia," which she did to everyone's delight except that of the officer from Georgia.

One amazing characteristic of the Irish people was their intense addiction to riding bicycles. Hampered by a lack of cars and gasoline, small children, old men, and women alike had adapted themselves to riding bicycles for all occasions. All five of our Company H officers rented bicycles from McSorley's Bicycle Shop. We used them like the natives for all our transportation needs.

Food in Northern Ireland was scarce. The only plentiful items were fish and chips augmented by plenty of Old Bushmills Irish Whiskey. Candy, meat, and clothing were severely rationed. Oranges, apples, and grapes could not be bought for any price. Occasionally we received a small ration of Coca-Cola, which sold for fifty cents per six-ounce bottle.

During the months of June and July the weather continued "unusual." The local people used this term to explain "the rainiest summer in fifty years." During this time the three battalions of the 135th Infantry were scattered over a wide area with distances of from ten to twenty miles separating them. The first battalion was at Ashbrooke, the second at Omagh, and the third at Colebrook. Each battalion conducted its own training with little supervision from our regimental headquarters.

By 1 July we had conducted extensive firing of mortars, rifles, and machine guns. We had received training in squad, platoon, and company tactics, and were physically hardened by our daily hikes of fifteen or more miles each afternoon. We were now ready for Exercise Atlantic, a ten-day maneuver against two British infantry divisions and the American First Armored Division, which simulated a Nazi invasion from the southeast.

Chapter VI
Exercise Atlantic

On 1 July the three infantry regiments of the Thirty-fourth Division moved by rail to a concentration area near Dungannon where the 135th Infantry was in division reserve for one day. On 2 and 3 July, we marched all day in a chilling rain.

On 4 July we made a forced march of thirty-five miles in an incessant downpour of cold rain. Although I wore heavy woolen clothing, which included a woolen overcoat and an allegedly waterproof raincoat, I was soon soaked to the skin, thoroughly chilled, and overcome with exhaustion. So was everybody else in the battalion.

Besides my heavy waterlogged clothing, I carried a nine-pound rifle, a bayonet, binoculars, and a heavy musette bag. The enlisted men carried even heavier loads. After twenty-five miles of this endless plodding through the rain, blisters the size of fifty-cent pieces formed on each of my feet, but I dared not quit hiking because I realized that if my exhausted men were to see me fall by the wayside, they would promptly do likewise, as so many men in other platoons of the battalion were doing when their platoon sergeants or platoon leaders quit because they couldn't take it any longer.

When I observed that some of my men were much more exhausted than I, I noticed also that many of them limped and staggered as if each step would be their last. This called for drastic action. Immediately, I increased my already pronounced limp and started groaning and gasping for breath, meanwhile complaining

and griping louder than anyo
effect of these actions was in
quickly offered to carry my rif
and platoon sergeant urged m
but I assumed the heroic ex
plodding forward at the head
the rumor spread among the th
lieutenant was in mighty bad s
dead any minute, but by G——
not fall out, they were not goi

Thus it came about tha
platoon completed a thirty-fi
worst possible weather witho
platoons of the battalion wher
percent of their men immediat
the firm leadership of junior o
thus clearly demonstrated.

When we finally made c
was 2000 hours. We had hiked
rest. Our supper consisted of s
Spam, and one with cheese—

Although the rain had te
ocean of mud and the water fe
Other than the large beech tr
cut, there was no wood to bui
windy night air. We flouted re
of beech limbs going full bla
and coffee soon chased away

On the fifth day of the
defensive position with small
posted at strategic road inters
pany H Command Post was
center of a circle of scatter
darkness "enemy tanks" infilt

Foll
entire wee
ment, and
by the me
of designa
censoring
week wa
administra
the follow
wrote imr

Durir
the length
hikes we
of Aberco
included
constitute
huge and

The g
invited the
us on a tou
hundreds

The
extensive
profusion,

Durir
battalion o
three traini
division p
these cente
as defendi
by artillery
attacks, wi
ous with n
the first we

served to add realism to the maneuvers, as did the ensuing transportation tie-up that added difficulty to our hauling ammunition and feeding us at least two hot meals daily.

During August we heard a rumor that the Allies had invaded France and all Canadian, British, and American troops were to be ready for immediate shipment to France. However, we had no official confirmation of any such alert. We did not have radios or other means of receiving news. The rumor was probably the distorted report of the Dieppe raid, which took place in August 1942.

That same afternoon I received an urgent message to report with all my equipment to headquarters, 168th Infantry, and learned that I was to accompany this unit as an observer on a highly secret mission to Inveraray, Scotland.

Chapter VII
Inveraray, Scotland

Also included in the group of six junior officers who made the trip to Inveraray were First Lieutenants Lyons, Greller, Ondecker, Openshaw, and Second Lieutenant Perry. Of the group of six, I was the only one who was not later killed, seriously wounded, or captured by the Germans.

At 2200 hours on 11 August, I was attached to the First Battalion, 168th Infantry, under the command of Lieutenant Colonel Baer and further assigned to Company D under the command of Capt. Floyd Sparks. We proceeded by truck in the darkness to Belfast and, after a short water trip, landed the next day at the fishing village of Inveraray, Scotland, on Loch Fyne, an estuary of the Fyne River near Loch Lomond.

Although our first glimpse of Scotland disclosed steep forest-clad slopes extending almost straight up from the sea for several hundred feet, the sunshine by day, the brilliant moon at night, and the absence of a chilling wind at all times was like going suddenly from winter to summer.

We were quartered near the outskirts of Inveraray in Quonset huts scattered on the broad acres of the duke of Argyle. On the first Sunday after our arrival in Scotland, several other lieutenants and I walked along the road in front of the duke's huge and beautiful old castle. As we stopped briefly to admire and stare at such a splendid view the duke of Argyle, himself, an elderly gentleman with silver-gray hair and a colorful kilt, suddenly appeared in the doorway of the castle's main entrance. To our surprise he called to us and beckoned us to come inside his castle. Then he graciously invited us to accompany him on an extremely interesting and informative tour of the many beautiful rooms and splendid halls of the entire castle. Among other items of interest he showed us many ancient suits of well-preserved armor and the bed in which Harriet Beecher Stowe slept in during her nineteenth century visit to Scotland.

After our delightful visit with the duke of Argyle, we plunged into an extremely gruelling program of commando training. This training, which was the best organized and the most realistic we had yet received, was supervised by young battle-trained British Commando officers, many of whom had seen bloody action at the Lofoten Islands in Norway and the Dieppe raid in France. Among these officers was a Lieutenant Colonel Churchill, who had a large dent in his helmet and insisted on carrying a huge saber that had been used by his grandfather in the Boer War and his father in World War I.

For three weeks, including Sundays, we worked from early morning until late afternoon, and often a large part of the night, with little rest. Following the usual hikes and calisthenics, we practiced loading and unloading from small landing boats, always jumping into the cold water deep enough to get wet to the waist in order to achieve realism. During the third week, we took afternoon hikes, walking one-half mile and running one-half mile up to distances of fifteen miles. We made several climbs up a sixty-degree slope to the top of a hill, at an elevation of a thousand yards, on top of which stood an old stone lookout tower that had been used to relay the news of the sinking of the Spanish Armada of Philip II of Spain by a storm off the Scottish coast in 1588. At night we practiced landing from the small boats, placing white tape on the backs of our helmets for identification and holding tightly to the man ahead to keep from getting lost.

Toward the end of the third week the First Battalion was loaded at night on the British army transport *Bulolo*. We were landed by small boats on the nearby coast and then made a twenty-five mile forced march across a barren, steep, and rocky mountain to the edge of a large lake. We encountered heavy "enemy" opposition, firing blank ammunition all the way, and finally arrived at the edge of the lake in late afternoon where we occupied a battalion defensive position all night. We were anticipating an attack by the British Commandos, who were scheduled to make a night assault from the water in small craft under Lieutenant Colonel Churchill.

This the Commandos did with such stealth that they achieved complete surprise by bursting upon us in unexpected howling, bloodcurdling fury. As a penalty for our failure, we had to reenact the entire problem, which required three more days of hardship.

Our regimental commander at that time was Col. John W. ("Iron Mike") O'Daniel, who had won his bars as a second lieutenant in World War I. Although he enforced discipline, there wasn't anything he wasn't willing to do to better the conditions of those serving under his command. He set a fine example of plain talk and direct action.

Although most of our time in Scotland was occupied with hard work, there was always time to attend occasional dances, several of which were held near our camp.

The unique Scotch dancing was not like anything I had seen before. The Scotch girls put American jitterbug to shame. (This was before our modern era of rock and roll.) The dancing tempo was much faster than jitterbug, accompanied by wild Indian war whoops and the shouts and yells of an old-time religious revival, with elements of the Virginia reel thrown in. The music gradually rose in tempo and intensity to a crescendo of rhythmic beats surpassing "In the Mood" or "Tiger Rag." Meanwhile, the young women and their kilted escorts yelled and whooped and leaped high into the air in perfect rhythm to the unearthly beat of the music until they fell utterly exhausted in crumpled heaps in the middle of the dance floor.

There was much optimism among our troops at that time about an early end to the war in Europe. Second Lieutenant Perry offered to bet me the sum of twenty dollars that the European war would end by 1 September 1943. I accepted the bet, but never collected my winnings as he was later captured by the Germans and I never saw him again. At that time, I predicted that the war in Europe would end on 1 September 1945.

On 15 September 1942 all personnel of the 135th Infantry were assembled and told that we would return to our outfits immediately, but under no circumstances were we to tell anybody, not even our commanding officers or fellow soldiers, where we had been or what we had been doing, on penalty of immediate court-martial and dishonorable discharge from the army.

Chapter VIII

Final Training for a Top Secret Voyage

After a short journey over water by night, I arrived in Ireland to find that my outfit had moved south from Omagh to the edge of the large lake resort, Ely Lodge. After staying there for only three days with my unit, I moved with the Second Battalion to another location a few miles to the east, called Camp Blessingbourne, near the small village of Fivemiletown.

Our stay at Camp Blessingbourne was quite uneventful. We conducted the usual training schedule of range firing, long marches, and small maneuvers. The local farmers still continued to gather on Saturday P.M., which was called Fair Day, into the center of town with their horses, pigs, sheep, and cattle inside a milling throng that blocked traffic for the entire day. The residue left in the streets after such a day was ample to enrich many a farmer's unfertile acre.

During this period, we were quartered in the usual Quonset tin roof huts on the estate of General Montgomery. The only thing that was unusual about our life was the "unusual weather," which continued to be even more unusual than usual. The chill of the winds increased in intensity, the clouds became grayer, and the size and frequency of the raindrops increased with the approach of autumn. The sun, moon, and stars seldom appeared. The only visible color was that of the leaves on the trees, which were slowly changing from green to red, gold, and orange. The little coal potbellied stoves in our huts had to be fed constantly to make them heat the farthest parts of our rooms.

At 2200 hours on 14 October, I was dozing in a chair beside

the stove in my quarters when the nearby telephone rang. Upon answering it, I received the information from Sergeant Bradford of Company H that I was hereby notified of my transfer to Company K, 135th Infantry, as a rifle platoon leader, effective at 1800 hours on 14 October 1942 and that I must report as soon as possible the next morning to my new company commander, Capt. Paul F. Thaler.

The following morning I reported to Colebrook to Lt. Col. Robert P. Miller, the commanding officer of the Third Battalion, 135th Infantry, who instructed me to report at once to Captain Thaler. I was assigned to duty as platoon leader of the Second Platoon. The other officers in the company were 2d Lt. John W. Flynn, Third Platoon leader; 1st Lt. Leo Voss, First Platoon leader; and 2d Lt. Luther L. Doty, Fourth Platoon leader. The executive officer and second in command of the company was 1st Lt. Tom Chegin. The first three platoons of Company K were armed with M-1 rifles and were designated as rifle platoons, whereas the Fourth Platoon was armed with 60-mm mortars and light machine guns.

Shortly after my arrival, Lt. Col. Edwin T. Swenson was placed in command of the Third Battalion. This colorful officer was an energetic, dynamic individual from Stillwater, Minnesota, who had established a solid reputation as a leader through his many years of experience in successfully handling men as the warden of a famous state penitentiary. Although, to the best of my knowledge, none of us were hardened criminals, all of us soon learned to respect Lieutenant Colonel Swenson for the vigor of his personality, his forthright manner, his keen sense of humor, and ready wit, and because he exercised his leadership through personal example rather than by trying to drive his subordinates.

On 18 October, the Third Battalion was suddenly moved from Colebrook to Sunnylands Camp near the seaport town of Carrick-fergus, near the city of Belfast, and we were informed that we would soon embark aboard two British destroyers, HMS *Malcolm* and HMS *Broke*, on a highly secret invasion mission. As a counterintelligence measure, word was promptly given out to the other two battalions of the 135th Infantry Regiment that the Third Battalion had departed to engage in an extended field exercise and maneuvers in the Sperrin Mountains north of Lough Neagh, the largest lake in Ireland.

During the seven days of our stay at Sunnylands Camp, we engaged in an intensive training program that stressed rough-and-tumble fighting and individual combat proficiency with the knife, the bayonet, and the grenade. To assist us in carrying out our mission, which had not been disclosed to us, some sixty British naval officers and men were attached to our battalion and furnished with U.S. Army uniforms to deceive our enemy as to their true identity. Several joint British-American boarding party teams were organized and trained thereafter in the specialized techniques of boarding small enemy ships. Lt. Col. Swenson supervised this training with a skeleton battalion staff consisting of Capt. Wilhelm Johnson, surgeon; Capt. William F. Snellman, executive officer; and Capt. Emory J. Trawick, communications officer. No chaplain was provided.

As part of our training, we were loaded on large trucks late each afternoon and transported during daylight to the Belfast dock area with our arrival timed to take place just before darkness. We were then unloaded from our trucks and promptly climbed on them again to return to our camp after darkness. This action was taken both to train us and to deceive the local people as to the exact hour of our departure. As a matter of fact we were deceived ourselves, for none of us knew when we would depart nor any specific facts about our destination or our mission. Finally, however, the veil of secrecy was partially lifted on the evening of 25 October, when, as a climax to our training, we engaged in a practice loading exercise by going aboard the destroyers *Malcolm* and *Broke* and assuming our positions, which presumably we would occupy during our secret mission.

Early on 26 October, we were awakened several hours before daylight and climbed aboard our trucks to make the familiar journey to the Belfast docks with all our baggage, equipment, and weapons. Upon arriving at the docks, another surprise awaited us. Instead of going aboard the two British destroyers, we embarked aboard the British cruiser *Sheffield*, one of the finest of its kind in His Majesty's Royal Navy. Altogether, twenty-one officers and 613 enlisted men of the Third Battalion, 135th Infantry, embarked on the *Sheffield*. These were in addition to two officers and fifty enlisted men of Company M who had already gone on board the preceding night, thus bringing the grand total for our Third Battalion to 686 officers and men on the *Sheffield*.

During the afternoon of 26 October we set sail on a voyage that initially was pleasant and singularly uneventful. In sharp contrast to the cold, cloudy climate of Northern Ireland, the weather throughout our voyage was warm, fair, and dry, with enemy submarines and aircraft conspicuous by their absence.

Chapter IX
Invasion!

For two days the *Sheffield* forged at full speed in a southeasterly direction through the sunny Atlantic Ocean. On our second night out of Belfast we joined a large convoy of aircraft carriers and troop transports heavily laden with American soldiers, planes, and landing craft of varied sizes and shapes. Thereafter, the *Sheffield* accompanied the convoy as a part of its naval escort.

Not until the third day of our voyage did we receive the slightest inkling of our destination or our mission. This secrecy was essential because our projected route included a twenty-four-hour stop in the port of Gibraltar. Finally, on 29 October, upon orders of Captain Fancourt of the Royal British Navy, all American and British officers on board assembled in the ship's wardroom (officers' lounge). To each of us the British naval captain gave a large scale map that showed in great detail the harbor and port installations of a French city, but from which all marks of identification had been carefully clipped out.

Midst an atmosphere of hushed expectancy, Captain Fancourt then told us that the Third Battalion, 135th Infantry, with its attached British naval personnel had been designated as the "Terminal Force" and placed under his command to participate shortly in a decisive action as a part of a grand Allied strategic offensive soon to be launched and that this offensive was expressly planned "to open the Mediterranean Sea to Allied ships, to chase the German army out of Africa, to knock Italy out of the war, and to shorten the ultimate length of the war in Europe by at least two years." In

34

concluding his remarks, he told us that we would remain on board the *Sheffield* until after our passage through the Strait of Gibraltar, after which we would transfer at sea to the destroyers *Malcolm* and *Broke*, in order to accomplish a mission which Lieutenant Colonel Swenson would now explain to us.

Lieutenant Colonel Swenson then gave us the general plan for the attack of the Third Battalion as follows. (For detailed orders and maps concerning this attack, see Appendices A, B, and C.)

Upon arriving within two days' journey of Gibraltar, the *Sheffield* would increase her speed, push out ahead of the convoy, and rendezvous with the destroyers *Malcolm* and *Broke* in the Mediterranean Sea, somewhere east of the Strait of Gibraltar. At the rendezvous area, Company K and the first two platoons of Company I would board the *Malcolm*, while the rest of Company I and all of Company L would board the *Broke*. The attached medical personnel and the heavy weapons personnel from Company M would be divided equally between the two destroyers.

After our transfer from the *Sheffield* to the two destroyers, the Terminal Force was to move at top speed to the French city shown, but not named, on our maps and then to ram a hole through the heavy steel antisubmarine boom stretched across the city's harbor entrance in order to land the American troops on the docks to prevent sabotage to the port installations. In approaching and ramming the boom, the *Broke* was to precede the *Malcolm* by a time interval of fifteen minutes.

From our maps it appeared that the city, which we were soon to attack, was situated on fairly level ground near the harbor, which rose sharply to the west into a series of rounded hills and steep ridges with heights in excess of two hundred meters (about 660 feet) above the level of the Mediterranean Sea. The harbor of the city was shaped like a large crescent with the open side facing to the east. It was protected from the open sea by artificially constructed breakwaters, or *jetées*, which jutted out to sea for distances of two-to three thousand yards. According to our intelligence reports, these *jetées* were solid concrete walls with an average height above the water of from five to ten feet. Several large piers, which in French were called *môles*, jutted from the shore far out into the harbor. From north to south these *môles* were (in order) *Môle Lyvois, Môle de Peche, Môle al Djefna, Môle des Passageurs, Môle al Mouchez, Môle aux Minerais, Grand Môle, Môle Louis Billiard.*

The objectives of the Third Battalion extended from the port offices and graving docks near *Môle al Mouchez*, south along the shore to the *jetée, Brise Lames Est*, a total distance of over three thousand yards. These objectives were to be attained by having the two destroyers ram a hole through the steel boom stretched across the entrance to *Bassin de Mustapha*, from *Jetée de Mustapha* to the north end of *Brise Lames Est.*

When I suddenly noticed on my map that the harbor was defended by several shore batteries of artillery, I forgot all about such things as *jetées* and *môles*. Our map clearly indicated that these batteries could inflict heavy casualties on us if the French offered determined resistance to our attack. I noted that the *Batterie des Arcades* located south and west of the harbor on a small rounded hill about one hundred meters (about 328 feet) high, could probably cover most of the harbor with fire. It also seemed that the batteries on *Jetée du Nord* and *Ilot de la Marine* could inflict severe damage on us as we entered the harbor. Captain Fancourt relieved our fears with the statement that picked British Commandos were assigned missions of capturing all these batteries before the scheduled time of our landings. It was also calculated that the batteries on *Jetée du Nord* and *Ilot de la Marine* could not be depressed enough to fire accurately over the seemingly effective barrier of the *jetées* to the south.

In attempting to evaluate the character of the ground on which our objectives were situated, we were handicapped by our lack of trained aerial photograph interpreters. Several distinct features on our aerial photo maps appeared to our untrained eyes to be positive enemy gun locations, but later after our landing when we inspected them at close range, they turned out to be large outdoor latrines, or *toilettes*.

Since our landings were scheduled for two hours after two other large friendly forces were to land respectively on two beaches east and west of the city of ———, from whence they were to execute a simultaneous sweeping double envelopment of the city, it was anticipated that we would probably meet little or no resistance from our enemy since most of the enemy troops defending the harbor would immediately be withdrawn to meet the threats from both flanks of the city.

The detailed attack plan of the Terminal Force consisted of three modifications of the same overall scheme of maneuver. In our field order for the executions of our amphibious assault, these modifications had been designated as Plans A, B, and C, respectively. (For details and map of this scheme of maneuver, see Appendices A and B and Map 3 in Appendix C.)

Plan A was to be executed in the happy event that both the *Malcolm* and the *Broke* should succeed in passing through the boom. It provided that the *Broke* would debark her troops (the Broke Force) directly onto the *Quai de Dieppe*. First Platoon, Company L, had a mission of capturing *Môle Louis Billiard* and the adjoining electric power station. The Second Platoon, Company L, had a mission of capturing Morey's Oil Depot near the power station. The Third Platoon, Company L, was to capture the small seaplane base west of the oil depot and then make contact with Company I at the base of the *Grand Môle*. The two platoons of Company I, which were aboard the *Broke*, the Fourth Platoon (weapons platoon) of Company L, and the heavy weapons troops of the Broke Force were to remain in mobile general support of the entire Broke Force from positions near the base of the *Grand Môle*. The Broke Force was to make contact with Company K on its right and then organize its objectives for defense against attack from the south and west.

Also, as a part of Plan A, the *Malcolm* was to follow the *Broke* by fifteen minutes and berth alongside the *Grand Môle*, landing her troops (the Malcolm Force) directly on the docks. The Second Platoon, Company K, commanded by 1st Lt. Leslie W. Bailey, was then to run at top speed along the shore and capture the port offices, the graving docks, and *Môle al Mouchez* on the extreme north flank of the battalion. The Third Platoon, Company K, commanded by 2nd Lt. John W. Flynn, had a mission of seizing the *Môle aux Minerais*. The First Platoon, Company K, commanded by 1st Lt. Leo Voss, had the mission of capturing the *Grand Môle* and of effecting a junction with the Broke Force on the south. The Fourth Platoon (weapons platoon), Company K, commanded by 2nd Lt. Luther L. Doty, and the remainder of the Malcolm Force were to stay in mobile supporting positions near the base of the *Grand Môle*. Immediately upon occupying their positions, the Malcolm Force was to organize all its objectives for defense against counterattacks from the north and west.

Plan B was predicted on the eventuality of success for the Broke Force in conjunction with failure of the Malcolm Force. By this plan, the Broke Force was to seize the objectives of the Malcolm Force in addition to their own.

Plan C provided for success of the Malcolm Force and failure of the Broke Force. In this eventuality, the Malcolm Force was required to seize the objectives of both forces.

The fourth eventuality, which was a part of all plans, provided for failure of either or both forces to hold their objectives after a successful landing had been effected. In this contingency, if a withdrawal became necessary because of overwhelming resistance or counterattack too strong to repel, three long blasts on the siren of either destroyer was the signal for its respective landing force to execute a retrograde movement and reembark on the destroyers, which would immediately put back out to sea.

In conjunction with all plans, the joint British-American boarding parties were to seize as many ships, which were already in the harbor, as possible.

We were instructed not to shoot unless fired upon, but if heavy resistance was met, the *Sheffield* and other heavy warships of the British Mediterranean Fleet would give us prompt naval gunfire support.

On 5 November, we paused for a few hours at Gibraltar, but no one wearing a United States Army uniform was permitted to go ashore or even to appear on any deck from where he could be observed from shore, any nearby ship, or other possible external observation point. We were, however, permitted to borrow British naval uniforms to wear long enough to move freely on the upper decks. In my case I borrowed the blue uniform of a first lieutenant of the British Royal Marine Corps. In this manner I was wearing proper insignia of my grade and this enabled me and most of the other U.S. soldiers aboard the *Sheffield* to get an excellent view of the Rock of Gibraltar on a bright, clear day.

After our departure from Gibraltar during the afternoon of 5 November 1942, we were told that our destination was the large city of Algiers on the Mediterranean coast of French North Africa. Maps and detailed plans for our attack were issued to all noncommissioned officers down to and including assistant squad leaders. In addition to the information that pertained directly to our mission, the officers were also filled in on some highly interesting background information about which we had heretofore known nothing.

We were told that in July 1942 at a conference in Washington between President Roosevelt and Prime Minister Churchill, the two Allied leaders had decided to make an amphibious invasion of North Africa instead of a direct attack on Europe across the English Channel. This attack against French North Africa was scheduled for November 1942 in conjunction with a determined drive westward by the British Eighth Army in Egypt with the ultimate objective of clearing North Africa of all Axis troops.

We were also told that if our landings at Algiers were successful, along with similar landings at other strategically located points on the North African Coast, this gigantic enterprise, which was appropriately named Operation TORCH, would accomplish results of far-reaching significance to the success of the Allied war effort against the Axis powers. Among other things, our success would result in the following.

1. Allied convoys could move freely in the Mediterranean Sea protected by land-based aircraft and could reach Egypt, Suez, and India without making the ten-thousand mile journey around the Cape of Good Hope.
2. Occupation of French North Africa by the Allies would complete the blockade of the Axis powers.
3. It would enable the Allies to hit directly at the soft underbelly of Europe by giving them advanced bases from which an invasion could be launched to knock Italy out of the war.
4. It would secure North Africa, Suez, and the Middle East from possible invasion through Spain by Axis forces.
5. Dakar would no longer be a threat to South America.
6. The French army could be reanimated and reequipped for active operations in driving the Nazi invaders from France.
7. It would force the Germans to send some combat divisions from the Russian front to North Africa and thereby relieve pressure from the Russian army then engaged in the heroic defense of Stalingrad.

At the time Operation TORCH was being planned, French North Africa was not an active theater of combat for American troops. Accordingly, the feelings of the local people were considered to be favorable toward the people of the United States.

Conversely, the French people of North Africa were deeply embittered at the British because of the combat action of the British navy against the French navy at Dakar and Oran immediately after the fall of France. Although the British had taken this action to prevent the Nazis from seizing the French fleet, it nevertheless strained relations between the two former allies almost to the breaking point. Because of the delicacy of these relations, it had been decided that the British navy should furnish only naval vessels and naval personnel to implement Operation TORCH, while the assault landing forces, except for several British Commando units, were to be furnished entirely by the United States.

These combined British and American land, sea, and air units were organized into three separate task forces placed under the overall command of Lt. Gen. Dwight D. Eisenhower, U.S. Army. The three task forces were assigned respective missions of striking simultaneously at the French North African port cities of Casablanca, Oran, and Algiers. (See Map 1, Appendix C.)

The Western Task Force, comprising some thirty-four thousand troops, under the command of Maj. Gen. George S. Patton, Jr., was to sail from the United States and seize the important naval base of Casablanca on the northwest coast of French Morocco.

The Central Task Force, comprising approximately thirty thousand U.S. troops, under command of Maj. Gen. Lloyd Fredendall, was to embark from the British Isles and capture the port of Oran and adjacent airfields on the Mediterranean coast of western Algeria.

The Eastern Task Force, comprising about forty-two thousand American and British troops, under the command of Gen. K. A. N. Anderson of the British army, was given the mission of capturing the city of Algiers. Within the Eastern Task Force, the assault troops were designated as the Eastern Assault Force and were placed under the direct command of Maj. Gen. Charles W. Ryder, U.S. Army, second in command to General Anderson and also commanding general of the Thirty-fourth U.S. Infantry Division, a part of which had remained in Northern Ireland and another part of which was participating in the actions of the Eastern Assault Force.

The Eastern Assault Force consisted of the Thirty-ninth Regimental Combat Team (roughly four thousand troops) from the U.S. Ninth Infantry Division; the 168th Regimental Combat Team (roughly four thousand troops) from the U.S. Thirty-fourth Division; our previously mentioned Third Battalion of the 135th Infantry Regiment; also from the Thirty-fourth Division, one battalion of American Rangers; and some British Commando units. Each of these units was to take part in the assault landings on Algiers at approximately 0100 hours, 8 November 1942, except that the Terminal Force, as previously stated, was to land some two hours after the other troops of the Eastern Assault Force had gone ashore.

The Thirty-ninth Regimental Combat Team was to land fifteen miles east of Algiers at Ain Taya and seize the airfield at *Maison Blanche*. (See Map 2, Appendix C.)

The 168th Regimental Combat Team was to land on beaches near Sidi Ferruch, about fifteen miles west of Algiers, make an overland march to positions on the outskirts of the city and capture the high ground, which dominates the city from the west.

The Ranger Battalion was to seize Fort Sidi Ferruch, west of Algiers.

The British Commandos were to seize several important coast artillery batteries, which dominated the harbor at Algiers, thereby preventing the French naval personnel who manned them from firing on our landing forces.

As has previously been narrated, the Third Battalion, 135th Infantry of the Thirty-fourth Division, as a part of the Terminal Force and in conjunction with landings of the foregoing forces, was to make a frontal assault landing on the port installations of the harbor at Algiers by debarking directly on the city docks, respectively from the British destroyers *Malcolm* and *Broke*.

Upon receiving so much background information concerning the grand strategic objectives of the huge mission of which we were such a small part, many of us were awed into silence, whereas others were filled with renewed patriotism and pride, while still others engaged in wild speculation, conjecture, and animated conversation.

However, we had but little time to speculate, since our voyage on the *Sheffield* was rapidly drawing to a close. At about 1630 hours on 6 November, the *Malcolm* came alongside the *Sheffield* and the Malcolm Force went aboard the destroyer without incident. The transfer of personnel to the *Broke* was made in like manner at about 1730 hours. Lieutenant Colonel Swenson and Captain Fancourt went aboard the *Broke*, commanded by Commander Layard, British Navy. Captain Snellman, our battalion executive officer, boarded the *Malcolm*, commanded by Lieutenant Commander Sears of the British navy.

The decks of each destroyer were equipped with a belt of quarter-inch-thick armor plate, three feet high, extending around its perimeter to protect us from small arms fire as we approached the docks. Additionally, each destroyer was provided with an extra thickness of armor plate on its prow to facilitate cutting the boom as we entered the harbor of Algiers. Because of limited space, we all had to remain closely packed together on the weather deck of each destroyer.

The course of events proceeded smoothly on 6 and 7 November. We were ordered to lie down early on the evening of 7 November as the fulfillment of our mission required us to be awakened shortly before midnight.

We carried out our instructions and were awakened according to plan at about 2350 hours on 7 November and alerted to prepare for action. I noted that the night was slightly overcast and visibility was fair. There was no moon.

At about 0220 hours on 8 November, Captain Fancourt received a message by radio that the landings of the Eastern Assault Force were successful and that Terminal Force must prepare to proceed through the boom immediately.

We steamed for about one hour toward Algiers until the lights of the city were clearly visible a few hundred yards to our starboard. Upon our closer approach, we could see at irregular intervals the orange flashes of artillery fire temporarily lighting up the velvety blackness of the hills beyond the city. However, the artillery batteries within the city limits still remained silent. Suddenly, all lights in the city were extinguished leaving only the dim outline of the higher buildings visible through the dusky gloom of the moonless night. Immediately searchlights on *Ilot de la Marine* began to scan the harbor with their beams pointed seaward. (See Map 3, Appendix C.)

Both destroyers were now steaming at full speed toward what their commanders thought was the correct location of the boom, with the *Broke* leading the way. For a few minutes both destroyers succeeded in eluding the searchlight beams, which were now moving frantically back and forth in a crisscross pattern across the harbor from several different directions. The blinding glare of the searchlights soon threw both destroyers off course, causing them to head outside *Jetée de Mustapha* to the north. They were forced to turn seaward so they could swing around in a wide arc for another try at crashing through the boom. The *Broke* was still in the lead.

Meanwhile the searchlights converged on the *Malcolm*, which was taking a heavy shelling from the *Batterie des Arcades*.

The *Broke* made a second attempt to breach the boom, but missed again because of heavy fire from both the *Batterie des Arcades* and *Jetée du Nord*. Captain Fancourt then radioed the *Malcolm* to go in if she could. However, the *Malcolm* also missed the boom on its second attempt and, upon turning seaward again, received several hits from the *Batterie des Arcades*. Fire broke out on the *Malcolm* amidships and Captain Fancourt received a message stating that the *Malcolm* was badly hit, was unable to continue the action, and was trying to withdraw beyond range of the shore batteries.

During this violent action both destroyers were flying large, easily recognizable United States flags at the top of their masts, but this ruse had failed to deter the French defenders on shore from firing on what must have appeared to them as ships of the United States Navy.

The Action of the *Broke*

When he learned that the *Malcolm* had been knocked out of action, Captain Fancourt directed that Plan B be executed immediately and that the *Broke* make its third attempt to break the boom. However, the intensity of the fire from the shore batteries caused this third attempt to fail.

However, her undaunted crew, inspired by the steadfast determination and absolute fearlessness of Captain Fancourt, turned her around again for her fourth effort at breaking the boom. As the artillery shells and machine-gun bullets whizzed past her, the *Broke* steamed forward with a burst of irresistible speed, her guns blazing away in all directions, cut through the boom with hardly any sensation of hitting it, and proceeded toward the *Grand Môle* until Commander Layard noticed that this area was filled with many small enemy ships. He quickly changed course and berthed the *Broke* alongside the *Quai de Falaise* on *Môle Louis Billiard.* A small enemy vessel beside the *Grand Môle* suddenly delivered several bursts of .50-caliber machine-gun fire at the *Broke*. This fire wounded some of the British crew members. Heavy machine-gun fire was also received from other ships and from warehouses in the vicinity of the oil depot. The British sailors promptly returned the machine-gun fire from their Oerlikons, sank the small enemy vessel, and knocked out some of the enemy machine guns.

Although badly shaken by the heavy bombardment, the Broke Force troops recovered quickly and debarked onto the docks without undue difficulty. Within a few minutes they had seized and occupied *Môle Louis Billiard,* the electric power station, and Morey's Oil Depot. Whether they would be able to extend north and seize the objectives assigned to the Malcolm Force was altogether dependent on the intensity of the resistance encountered in that direction.

It was now about 0530 and daylight was fast approaching. Utmost speed was essential to organize the newly won positions for effective resistance against almost certain counterattack by the enemy. Initially, enemy automatic weapons fire directed at street intersections and open lanes in the vicinity of the landing area was ineffective. However, with the arrival of daylight, enemy machine-gun fire began to hit among our troops from several different directions.

Despite this heavy fire, our troops continued to consolidate their positions until about 0800 hours, when two policemen and two civilians under the protection of a white flag contacted some of our troops. They asked Lieutenant Colonel Swenson to send an emissary with them to arrange for the formal surrender of Algiers to the U.S. forces on the docks. Meanwhile, one of the British navy boarding party commanders informed Lieutenant Colonel Swenson that a French army officer had contacted him and told him the Broke Force was almost surrounded by French troops definitely opposed to cooperating with the Americans.

Before Lieutenant Colonel Swenson could make a decision, several rounds of artillery from the direction of *Jetée du Nord* landed in the area. The third round passed through the bow of the *Broke* and forced her to move to a position beside the *Quai de Dunkerque*. Artillery fire completely covered the area between the landed area and the *Broke*, destroying all wire communication between them. The situation became even more desperate when the *Batterie des Arcades* suddenly adjusted its fire on the *Broke* and, after delivering six rounds, scored five direct hits.

One of these rounds passed through the Medical Aid Station on the *Broke* causing heavy casualties among both British and Americans. The British junior medical officer was instantly killed and the senior medical officer had his right arm blown off. An American medical aid man, Private Tellas, with a display of unusual courage and tenacity of purpose assumed the duties of the surgeon. Under the direction and supervision of the senior medical officer, who kept himself conscious by self-administered morphine, Private Tellas miraculously performed several amputations of arms and legs and opened up abdomens, thus saving many lives. (For this extraordinary coolness under fire, Tellas received the American Silver Star Medal; a citation from His Majesty, the king of England; and a scholarship in medicine at a university in the United States.)

In view of the increased volume and accuracy of the artillery fire, Captain Fancourt decided that the *Broke* must leave Algiers immediately or be sunk. Accordingly, he directed that the ship's siren sound the prearranged signal for immediate withdrawal of the landed troops.

When Lieutenant Colonel Swenson heard the recall siren he noted that it was about 0930. He opined that the regimental combat teams of the Eastern Assault Force should now be nearing the city and that, therefore, it ought to be possible for the Broke Force to hold out until the Eastern Assault Force troops arrived in the dock area to relieve his own beleaguered, greatly outnumbered, and weary troops. He decided that an attempt at withdrawal would inevitably result in heavy casualties and also in unnecessary delay for the *Broke*. He therefore ordered his men to remain on shore and to continue defending their positions.

Meanwhile Captain Fancourt was desperately trying to get the *Broke* out to sea beyond the range of the murderous shore batteries. Because of her badly damaged condition, it was necessary to have her taken under tow by another British destroyer, which was fortunately available from the British navy ships in the vicinity. After much difficulty, both destroyers cleared the harbor without being sunk.

During all this time, water continued to pour into the hold of the *Broke* through the many holes below her waterline. (According to a statement made later by Lieutenant Colonel Swenson, the *Broke* suffered twenty-two direct hits from the shore batteries, some of which were more than a foot in diameter.) Since the *Broke* was now on the verge of sinking, Captain Fancourt ordered all hands to abandon ship and to go aboard the destroyer that was towing them. Almost immediately after the last man was evacuated from the

Broke, she disappeared with a gurgle beneath the dark blue waves of the Mediterranean Sea, carrying with her all reserve mortar and small arms ammunition, as well as all personal equipment, clothing, and supplies of the troops whom she had debarked on the docks.

The Defense of the Docks

Meanwhile, on the docks the situation had improved slightly. The warehouses along the harbor contained bales of hay and miscellaneous goods that our troops used to construct breastworks behind which they organized a perimeter defense with all outside approaches covered by fire. At about 1100 hours, six Allied planes from our aircraft carriers dive-bombed the batteries on *Jetée du Nord* and *Ilot de la Marine* and succeeded in silencing them. Our troops now regrouped and poured a deadly fusillade of small arms and machine-gun fire into the ranks of the enemy.

However, because of the impending exhaustion of their ammunition without any hope of resupply, it was impossible for the Broke Force to keep up its heavy volume of fire on the enemy for much longer. Thus the tide of battle was about to turn in favor of the enemy.

With each passing second the situation of our troops became more critical. Shortly after 1130, some ten enemy Renault tanks circled the Broke Force and commenced pouring a heavy volume of machine-gun and shell fire into the American positions. This caused some casualties, in addition to setting on fire some of the baled hay that shielded the Americans. Also, the stacked mortar ammunition caught fire and commenced to explode, threatening the destruction of the entire dock area. Our infantry was without any artillery fire support; the promised naval gunfire support was not being received; and the battalion commander was unable to use either his mortars or his machine guns for fear of injuring the French women and children and inflaming the people of the city. Our troops were not provided with any antitank guns to destroy the tanks that were closing in from all sides of the perimeter. The Americans could not dig foxholes into the concrete pavements of the streets, nor could they retreat into the sea. Thus, it seemed that there was no means to escape the deadly fire of the enemy tanks that rained in their midst. Moreover, the absence of the sound of gunfire in other parts of the city indicated that disaster might have befallen the two United States regimental combat teams that should have long since arrived within the city limits of Algiers.

Rather than subject his gallant troops to almost certain annihilation with nothing to be gained thereby, Lt. Col. Edwin T. Swenson surrendered his positions and his entire force to the attackers at approximately 1230 hours on 8 November 1942.

The victorious French forces consisted of three companies of Senegalese infantrymen and one company of Mobilia Guardia naval troops, reinforced by twelve scout cars and tanks.

Immediately after their surrender, the American prisoners, with some attached British personnel, were lined up in the streets and disarmed. While the wounded men on both sides were being treated, the Senegalese troops commenced systematically to strip our troops of their rings, watches, and billfolds. Lieutenant Colonel Swenson protested vigorously at this outrageous conduct. At this juncture, the French commanding officer lined several of the vandals up and told the remainder of their Senegalese companions that he would shoot those he had lined up unless within two minutes all the personal belongings were returned to the Americans. This immediately accomplished its intended effect of quick restoration of the confiscated personal belongings to our men.

The U.S. and British officers were loaded on a huge van and taken to the Admiralty Offices on *Ilot de la Marine* for Intelligence interrogation. Almost immediately after their arrival, a French naval commander walked up to Lieutenant Colonel Swenson, arrogantly jabbed a .45-caliber pistol into his stomach and demanded harshly that information be given immediately concerning the plans of our Eastern Assault Force or else all the prisoners would be at once thrown into an underground dungeon. However, at this precise moment Capt. Viso Tangears, also of the French navy, arrived and roundly reprimanded all who had failed to render the utmost courtesy to the Allied officers. Thereafter, our officers were given comfortable quarters and also excellent food from the French officers' mess instead of the bucket of edible garbage that had been previously served to them. Meanwhile, the enlisted prisoners had been segregated from the officers and marched off to imprisonment in a nearby barracks.

Our officers were treated with great courtesy and consideration until the afternoon of 10 November 1942 when the city of Algiers finally capitulated formally to Maj. Gen. Charles W. Ryder, commanding general, Eastern Assault Force. As a part of the surrender agreement, our troops of the Broke Force were released immediately. However, the French never did restore the .45-caliber pistols to those of our officers who were armed with this type of weapon.

The Action of the *Malcolm*

One of the five-inch shells that hit the *Malcolm* amidships on her second attempt to ram through the steel chain boom exploded on contact with her smokestack and hurled shell fragments in all directions, causing heavy casualties (both killed and wounded) among the tightly packed troops on her decks. As she was hit again, the destroyer listed so violently to starboard that the waterline was only six inches below her weather deck. When a third shell arced downward through her center hatch and exploded in her boiler room, three of her four engines were badly damaged, her speed was reduced to only four knots, and a torrent of water commenced to pour through the holes that had been ripped in her sides.

Meanwhile the sparks from the exploding shells had ignited

the tarred pasteboard containers of a large pile of mortar ammunition stacked on her center hatch. Immediately bright crackling flames flared skyward sharply delineating the *Malcolm* against the ebony background of sky and sea.

The destroyer was now a perfect target to the French artillerymen who manned the coastal defense batteries on the hills surrounding Algiers. As one of the British sailors later expressed it, "The situation was just a bit sticky."

Shortly before the action commenced, I had received an order from Captain Thaler to move my platoon from the left side of the destroyer, where all the shells were now hitting, over to a position on its right side on that portion of the deck partially sheltered by the vertical part of the center hatch, so that we could debark faster to our objectives on the docks. During this violent action, several spent shell fragments hit my helmet and bounced off, causing me to make a frantic effort to claw with my fingernails through the steel floor of the deck. For a few moments I was torn with indecision as to whether I should remain where I was or jump overboard and take my chances on being rescued from the Mediterranean Sea.

Suddenly, 1st Lt. William E. Muir, of Company I, dashed forward with a display of extraordinary heroism and hurled several of the burning mortar cases over the deck rails into the sea. His prompt example inspired so many others to come to his assistance that only a few seconds were required to get rid of all the burning material and thus avert the certainty of a catastrophic explosion.

Only through the consummate skill and determination of her commander and crew was it possible to maneuver the *Malcolm* out to sea beyond the range of the shore batteries. When this was finally accomplished, the destroyer cruised slowly back and forth outside the harbor until dawn.

For several minutes after the shelling ceased, confusion reigned aboard the *Malcolm*. In the darkness, it was difficult to determine how many men had been killed and wounded. However, I soon discovered, with a chill of horror, that the platoon leader from another company, who had moved his platoon into the area so recently vacated by my platoon, had been killed along with several of his men. Neither I nor any of my men had been killed or wounded, but all of us were well aware that only the miracle of the order that moved the platoons had saved many of us from certain death.

As soon as possible after daylight, the wounded were treated, and the blood, brains, and tattered clothing were washed off the deck. Afterwards the bodies of the dead were placed in mattress covers and, in a sad but impressive mass funeral ceremony, were consigned to eternal rest beneath the waters of the Mediterranean Sea.

As soon as reorganization had been accomplished, the *Malcolm* pulled alongside the *Bulolo*, the headquarters ship of the invasion fleet, and all troops were permitted to go aboard her for a hot meal. As we stepped off the gangplank onto the deck of the *Bulolo*, a young Captain of Commandos, Randolph Churchill, the British prime minister's son, greeted us, threw his arm around Captain Thaler's shoulder and insisted on buying him a drink at the ship's officer's bar, which offer Captain Thaler quickly accepted.

After the rest of us had eaten a delicious dinner on the *Bulolo*, we returned to the *Malcolm* and prepared to go ashore by means of several small landing craft, which pulled alongside her to take us ashore. They made one trip to the beach with most of our troops; but on their return for the rest of us, they were tossed so violently by the rough waves that it was necessary to postpone the unloading until the next morning.

Late that afternoon German bombers made a determined attack on the invasion fleet but were driven off by antiaircraft fire. At daylight on 9 November, the enemy bombers returned but were driven off again.

Meanwhile, word had been received that Algiers had surrendered to U.S. troops and preparations were made for the *Malcolm* to enter the harbor immediately. However, this was impossible because of the heavy damage sustained by her engines. It was, therefore, late afternoon before hastily accomplished emergency repairs enabled her to start slowly toward the port. She had proceeded but a short distance when a large formation of JU-88 bombers suddenly attacked and scored several hits on the ships in the harbor. One ship was hit and damaged so badly that she burst into flames followed by several loud and rapid explosions. The attack was broken up by heavy antiaircraft fire and two British Spitfire fighter planes that swooped out of the clouds and immediately shot down one of the enemy craft. The German plane burst into a bright flame and spun crazily toward the water below accompanied by a thunderous clapping of hands and loud cheers from those aboard the *Malcolm*.

It was not until approximately 1000 hours on 10 November 1942 that I finally set foot on the shores of North Africa. I then learned that our troops from the *Malcolm*, who had debarked earlier, had been ordered to make a forced march of about ten miles into the city with full field packs and equipment. This march was accomplished successfully, but several men fell exhausted along the road because they had grown physically soft during the long sea voyage from Northern Ireland. Limited space on the *Sheffield* and the *Malcolm* had crowded them so closely together, adequate physical conditioning exercises had been impossible. These troops had been landed outside the city limits because of the uncertainty of the military situation within Algiers. However, they arrived on the scene of action in Algiers too late to assist in its capture. All organized resistance in the city had ceased at approximately 1900 hours (7:00 P.M.) on 8 November 1942.

Summary of Operations of the Terminal Force

The mission assigned to the Terminal Force was, by its very nature, almost impossible to accomplish. In some respects, it might well be compared to Pickett's Charge at Gettysburg, or to the charge of the Light Brigade at Balaclava. It was launched without the element of surprise, one of the nine commonly accepted principles of war. It violated a basic principle by pitting naval vessels against fixed harbor defense guns. This principle had been conclusively proved unsound by the disastrous consequences suffered by the vessels of the British fleet in the Dardanelles during the Gallipoli campaign of World War I.

In some respects the plan of attack of the Terminal Force was faulty. It assumed that the British Commandos would succeed in capturing the fixed harbor defense guns in Algiers and thus preclude their firing on the two destroyers. Thus, the success or failure of the plan hinged on the success or failure of the Commandos in capturing their objective. When, for reasons unknown, the Commandos failed to capture the shore batteries, the mission of the Terminal Force was almost doomed to failure. Also, the plan was faulty because of the assumption that the landing of two infantry regimental combat teams simultaneously on beaches fifteen miles away on each side of Algiers would, within two hours, draw so many enemy troops quickly out of the city that few or none of them would be left to oppose our landings on the docks. The plan was also faulty because it assumed that fire from heavy naval vessels of the British fleet would give us direct support. We never received any such support. Also, it appeared that the type of attack expected of the Terminal Force was faulty when compared directly to the outcome of a similar operation of the two British corvettes *Walney* and *Hartland* in their unsuccessful attempt to make a frontal assault on the harbor at Oran, on the night of 8 November 1942. The two small British ships also met overwhelming resistance from fixed shore batteries. In this action, both ships were sunk with some 189 killed and 157 wounded out of an attacking force of approximately 393.

In certain other respects, the plan of attack of Terminal Force and its execution had been admirable. On the battalion level, the plan was full, complete, and flexible, because the three alternatives, which it contained, provided all subordinate leaders with complete, detailed instructions on what they must do if certain sudden exigencies should develop during the execution of the attack. The cooperation of American and British forces at the battalion level left nothing to be desired. Captain Fancourt, Commander Layard, and Lieutenant Commander Sears had been remarkably cool and courageous during all phases of the attack. French naval commanders who observed the action later stated that whoever commanded the destroyer that broke the boom had accomplished a magnificent feat in naval operations.

Much credit must also be given to the officers, soldiers, and sailors who fought so gallantly on the docks. The tenacity, raw courage, aggressiveness, and skill that they displayed in seizing and holding their objectives under extremely hazardous conditions was in keeping with the finest military and naval traditions of Great Britain and the United States.

The quick decision of Lieutenant Colonel Swenson to forbid his troops to retreat to the *Broke* when the recall siren was sounded was basically a sound one. Such a retrograde movement would have invited disaster.

Also, the decision of the American battalion commander to surrender his troops to prevent useless sacrifice of American lives was sound. The overall plan for attacking the city specified that the 168th and Thirty-ninth Regimental Combat Teams would arrive in Algiers before noon. For this reason, the Terminal Force was provided with enough equipment, weapons, and supporting arms to withstand a sustained attack of but a few hours. Despite this limitation, it succeeded in its mission of preventing sabotage to port facilities because it held out three hours longer than originally anticipated. Also, as an unplanned contributing factor to its success, the French forces were so jubilant at forcing one-half of a heavily armed American infantry battalion to surrender, at successfully repelling the landing attempt of the other half of this same battalion, and at sinking one British destroyer and badly crippling another that they forgot all about sabotaging port facilities in Algiers. Their honor had been more than satisfied.

Thus, the Terminal Force had overcome almost insuperable obstacles by accomplishing the seemingly impossible task of making an unsupported frontal assault against fixed naval batteries that possessed vastly greater firepower than them. Moreover, the Terminal Force had seized and held its objectives for seven long, gruelling hours without any artillery support in an area where its troops were unable to dig foxholes to escape the heavy fire they received from many directions. During its relatively short engagement, the Third Battalion of the United States 135th Infantry Regiment had suffered casualties of fifteen killed and thirty-three wounded. The British naval forces accompanying us had suffered casualties of approximately twenty-five killed and twenty-five wounded. Thus, the aggregate casualties in killed and wounded for the Terminal Force were approximately one hundred. Enemy losses were an estimated seventy killed and one hundred wounded. By comparison, the Thirty-ninth Regimental Combat Team, a force vastly larger than the Terminal Force, had sustained casualties of two killed and ten wounded; and the 168th Regimental Combat Team of approximately the same size as the Thirty-ninth Regimental Combat Team had suffered casualties of ten killed and thirty-eight wounded.

In recognition of exemplary conduct and outstanding bravery under fire during its landing operations at Algiers, the commanding general of the Thirty-fourth Infantry Division designated the Third Battalion, 135th Infantry Regiment, as a Guard of Honor for Thirty-fourth Division formal affairs.

Chapter X
Palace Guards

For several days after going ashore in Algiers, we bivouacked on the docks near the edge of the harbor. Consequently we witnessed the tremendous amount of shipping and supplies that were being rushed to the British and American troops who were already racing to try to capture Tunis and Bizerte before the arrival of the Germans. We were assigned duties of assisting to unload the ships in the harbor and of furnishing guards and sentries for the buildings in the dock areas. Meanwhile, we continued to sleep on the hard concrete of the dock areas.

Algiers was a city of sharp contrasts. It was a fascinating metropolis where the customs and habits of a two-hundred-year-old civilization of the Arabs existed side by side with the highly civilized French residents of the city. The French section of the city along the Rue Michlet and the Rue Bab A'Zoun was a place of modern buildings and broad palm-lined streets, with beautiful terraced villas surrounded by beautiful lawns and groves of orange and lemon trees. The Arabs, comprising about 50 percent of the people, were located mainly in the Kasbah, an iniquitous, mysterious place of winding narrow streets, dirty buildings, and poverty-stricken people.

The typical Arab man was large, swarthy, and poorly clad, his attire consisting of either a red fez or a burnoose wound tightly about his head with a large dirty sheetlike robe wrapped round his body. The Arab women wore large white robes also and mantles that concealed their faces when they appeared in public. A stern warning was issued to the American soldiers to stay out of the Kasbah and not speak to the Arab women on penalty of subjecting ourselves to the swift retribution of terrible death at the hands of their brothers, husbands, or fathers.

Despite these warnings a few foolish soldiers ventured into the Kasbah and some of them were promptly involved in the scandalous revelries and drunken brawls as had been anticipated. It is questionable whether the soldiers or the Arab women were the aggressors in these cases inasmuch as many of the Arab women were addicted to whistling, whispering, and hissing every time a U.S. soldier passed near one of them in a frantic effort to attract his attention.

The Arabs, having been exploited for centuries, had developed an intense hatred of the French people, but they were neutrals between the Germans and Americans. Having been obsessed with war, bloodshed, and violence for centuries, they accepted invasion, bombing, and death as the normal course of events.

The only available means of transportation in the city consisted of the trolleybus, electrically driven streetcars similar to those in America, which for the sum of four cents (two francs) would take one anywhere in the city of over four hundred thousand people. The Arabs usually transported themselves by tiny donkeys harnessed to heavily loaded carts, which the Arabs forced the donkeys to pull by beating the animals unmercifully.

Our temporary location on the docks was wide open to German air attack for many days. Promptly at sundown, at sunrise, and often at noon, the German bombers made their appearance over Algiers and dropped bombs on the shipping in the harbor, necessitating our rapid entry into the air-raid shelters near the docks.

There were many outdoor cafes and restaurants in the French parts of the city. As Major Snellman, First Lieutenant Muir, and I made our way toward one of these on 10 November 1942, we had difficulty in fighting our way through the swarm of ragamuffin Arab urchins who beset us on every side and yelled in insistent tones,

"Gif me cigarette, chockolat, chowing gum." We cleared a path through them by throwing them a few cigarettes, which caused the howling, scratching mob to dive headlong into the gutter after them. Our wonder at this sight often turned to astonishment when smartly clad French men and women often joined in the spectacle and clawed and fought as violently as the children.

After seating ourselves in the cafe, we ordered a meal of tangerines, mutton, brown bread, and wine. The meal was well cooked and in delightful contrast to cold C rations. The cost of the meal was about forty cents each. I drank a lot of wine because I had observed the French people drinking it in such large quantities without any harmful effect. Afterwards I was barely able to walk to my bedding roll on the docks, about one-quarter of a mile away, before I collapsed in a heap, unable to remove my clothes or move a muscle until morning. It was a fortunate coincidence that the Germans failed to make their usual air raid that night.

We remained on the docks until 20 November when we moved to a large school building located not far away in the finest part of the city. The school had a large indoor courtyard covered with grass and bordered by orange and lemon trees. There was ample room for all our troops in the building and also for setting up our kitchens. Our diet consisted only of hash, stew, and beans supplemented by coffee and teeth-breaker biscuits, but we could now buy wine, fresh fruits, figs, and dates to augment our fare.

On 20 November I was ordered to report with my platoon to the Thirty-fourth Division Headquarters, situated on a high plateau on the western edge of the city in a beautiful marble building of Arabic architecture that had formerly been used as the German Consulate. This location gave us a good view of the entire city and the harbor.

I was told that my platoon would be the special guard and furnish all sentries for guarding Thirty-fourth Division Headquarters. On 22 November, Second Lieutenants Flynn and Doty joined me with their platoons and all three platoons were thereafter commanded by 1st Lt. Tom Chegin of Donora, Pennsylvania. At this time our company kitchen joined us and enough supplies were provided for us to eat palatable American food again. We were known thereafter as the Palace Guards.

From 22 November 1942 until 4 January 1943, we lived in a school building called L'École de Jeune Filles near Thirty-fourth Division Headquarters. Doty, Flynn, Chegin, and I occupied a small room that had been the office of *Le Directeur*, or superintendent of the school, a pleasant, middle-aged gentleman, who made a daily visit and insisted that we receive French language lessons every day. We were somewhat indifferent to the necessity of learning French until *Le Directeur* brought his pretty daughter with him. After that our progress in learning French increased so rapidly that we were soon reading French novels and speaking with the finesse and skill of a Parisian.

Across the hall from *Le Directeur's* office dwelt an aged French lady, her daughter, and little granddaughter Huguette, aged *neuf et demie,* nine and one-half years. With her pretty features, large brown eyes, olive complexion, silky brown hair, and affectionate nature, she immediately became the sweetheart of the Palace Guards. She was showered daily with small gifts of candy, C ration biscuits, and small sums of money. Her father had been killed in the war, a fact that elicited much sympathy from everyone.

Huguette's mother was soon doing a rushing business of washing, ironing, and sewing for 120 American soldiers.

American soldiers are by nature free-hearted and generous both with their possessions and money. The exercise of this trait by all soon resulted in all exits of the school building being constantly patrolled by a howling mob of tatterdemalions of all ages, sexes, and sizes who rushed up with tears in their eyes to every U.S. soldier they saw and begged for money, cigarettes, and food. If anything was given to one of them, he invariably fought like a wildcat and refused to give any to his fellows.

There was one pitiful case of an aged, bearded, one-legged

60

Arab who hovered persistently near the main door of the school building. Second Lieutenant Flynn gave him so much money he stated that he planned to list the old man on his income tax return the following year as a dependent.

Our duties of guarding division headquarters were so light that we had plenty of time for recreation. We had one day on duty followed by two days off duty during which we could go anywhere in the city, except to the Kasbah. Grapes, oranges, dates, and figs were plentiful in the city, in marked contrast to their complete absence in Ireland. The weather was warm and dry with plenty of sunshine, blue skies, and moonlit nights, also in marked contrast to the Irish weather. The rainy season started during the latter part of December, but we were quartered indoors with few outside duties.

Each night we were treated to a magnificent display of fireworks provided by the curtain of antiaircraft fire, which was thrown up to drive away the nightly twenty-five to one hundred German bombers. The planes came in from the west and swooped down toward the harbor from over the high ground. The fiery hail of antiaircraft shells, which mushroomed skyward from all parts of the city, was so effective that, in two months of steady bombing, the only harm done was the killing of a few Arabs, damage to some buildings along the waterfront, and the wounding of a few American soldiers from falling antiaircraft shell fragments. During the hours of daylight, a thick smoke screen shielded the ships in the harbor from the eyes of the attacking bomber pilots.

During December, we noted that events in Tunisia were not going according to plan. We surmised that we might soon be at the front. This did not leave much time to cultivate our slowly developing friendship with the Algerian people. In accordance with the customs of the local people, no nice French girl could be seen in public with a gentleman unless engaged to him or accompanied by the young lady's brother, father, or mother. A girl in Algiers could not dine in public unless chaperoned. To further complicate matters, no respectable French girl dared stay out later than 1900 hours.

61

Dancing was forbidden because the French were in mourning over the fall of France.

There were, however, plenty of girls who were more concerned with obtaining soap, cigarettes, and chocolate bars than with maintaining their reputations. They associated freely in public with the American soldiers.

Prices in Algiers rapidly rose to fantastic levels. Wine, which the French drank for breakfast, dinner, and supper, remained plentiful, but at much higher prices than when the U.S. troops first landed. I located a small restaurant owned by the self-styled *roi du base-ball* (the King of Baseball), a young Arab who had served three years in the American army in Panama and who insisted every time my friends and I dropped into his restaurant on setting us up with a free dinner of fried chicken, eggs, and champagne. We always paid for our meals over his protests, as we figured that he must surely have some ulterior motive behind his outward show of generosity.

Not far from our school building, several U.S. officers lived in the beautiful villa of the *Deux Frères*. It was surrounded by a high hedge and had a roof balcony, a pretty lawn, and lemon trees growing in the yard. It had a modern bathroom. The house was richly furnished and had beautiful pictures hanging on the walls. On the table in the dining room was a pretty music box. On it was the hand-painted picture of two happy children in a meadow on a bright summer day, chasing a butterfly.

Time seemed to pass rapidly. Almost before we knew it, it was Christmas Eve, and one of the enlisted men suggested that we arrange a Christmas party for Huguette.

It was a fine party. We invited all the French families in the vicinity. Our party started with a welcoming speech, which I gave in broken French. I attempted to explain what Christmas meant to American soldiers. Next we had some skits and harmonica playing by a group of men from Brooklyn. Accompanied by his guitar, a young soldier sang the following song.

"When Company K gets back to the U.S.A.
All the people will say, 'Hooray'
Oh what a *day* . . . when Company K
Gets back to the U.S.A."

After the music and some rather stale attempts at comedy, we joined in singing Christmas carols, such as "Silent Night" and "Hark! the Herald Angels Sing."

During the party, a group of soldiers slipped into the living room of Huguette's home and set up a Christmas tree, which they loaded with gifts of flour, canned meats, candy, soap, and C rations. Upon returning, Huguette's mother was so thrilled at our kindness that her eyes filled with tears and she made us accept a huge bowl of cookies she had baked for her own family to enjoy on Christmas Day.

Although German bombers roared over Algiers all night on Christmas Eve 1942, the men of Company K had learned the true meaning of Christmas in the simple act of giving and bringing happiness into the dreary life of a destitute French family.

On Christmas Day, 1st Lt. John Lyons, one of the officers from the villa of the *Deux Frères*, and I accepted an invitation from a French family to dine with them in their home. The French family consisted of a French gentlemen, Monsieur Lillo, his wife, a son, and two attractive daughters. Their home was located on a small farm of several acres.

Our dinner consisted of fried chicken, roast lamb, French bread, olives, tangerines, four different kinds of wine, and champagne. We presented Mr. Lillo with a quart bottle of Scotch whiskey and the rest of the family with a large box containing an assortment of soap, coffee, sugar, C rations, and candy, all scarce items in Algiers. During the dinner, the Frenchman drank so much wine and whiskey he became eloquent and stated that he ardently hoped for the annexation of the whole of North Africa by the United States government.

Following dinner, Mr. and Mrs. Lillo conducted us on a tour of the vineyards, the chicken roosts, and the orange groves. We enjoyed the Christmas dinner very much.

Chapter XI
Preparation for Combat

During the last few days of 1942, our daily news accounts from the war front in Tunisia conveyed the grim news that the Germans were steadily pushing the British First Army and the poorly armed, hastily organized, but brave French forces steadily to the rear. The Germans had already captured the large cities of Tunis and Bizerte and were now moving into the mountains south and west of the two cities. We surmised that Company K would soon take its place in the frontlines and that we would have but little time in Algiers to cultivate our slowly developing friendship with the local French and Arab people.

On New Year's Day 1943, we were informed that the remaining infantry regiment of the Thirty-fourth Infantry Division, which had remained in Northern Ireland since our amphibious assault on Algiers in November, had just landed in Oran, a few hundred miles to the west of us, and that we must get ready immediately to join them in order to train for combat service in Tunisia.

Early on the morning of 4 January, four large green buses waited outside our billets in L'École de Jeune Filles to receive us. Our Algerian friends stood with streaming eyes and sadly waved good-bye as we filed slowly out of the school building and climbed aboard the waiting buses. Huguette sobbed bitterly. *Le Directeur* shook hands warmly with as many of us as he could. Meanwhile, even among the ragamuffin Arab urchins, tears fell from many eyes as they set up a last frenzied screaming in mournful tones, "Cigarette! Chowing gum! Chocolat! Bonbon!"

Although the buses were crowded, we were soon settled down comfortably and travelling swiftly over the wild foothills of the Atlas Mountains west of Algiers. Throughout most of North Africa, the land rises steeply from the sea for several hundred feet then levels off into high arid land with sparse vegetation, inhabited chiefly by dirty, poorly clothed Arab nomads who dwell in small villages of dirty mud huts. Near the Mediterranean coast the rainfall is abundant, and the rich land is covered with green vineyards and orange groves extending as far as the eye can see.

Our route led over a winding road through a dense forest of evergreen trees, thence along the edge of an arid plateau and through rich farming country. The vineyards gave a brilliant green hue to the landscape. For many miles the road along the coast was broad and straight. The large farmhouses were constructed of cream-colored stucco, which made a pleasing contrast to the green of the vineyards, the yellow of the oranges, and the blue of the sky.

At the close of the first day, we bivouacked in an open field beside the highway to the right of the road in an isolated location to prevent the local populace from stealing everything we had. Because of the thin, dry air, the night was bitterly cold.

Our second day of travel led us through a thinly populated region where people were much poorer than those nearer Algiers. The land was rocky and large irrigation flumes paralleled the road.

During the afternoon of 5 January, we passed through Oran, the second largest city of Algeria. We continued beyond Oran to a rocky group of muddy hills near the village of St. Cloud. We bivouacked among some scraggly olive trees on a rock-strewn hillside. It was the middle of the rainy season, and our heavy trucks made the ground throughout the area a quagmire of mud. We pitched our pup tents in the mud and immediately stretched our weary bodies on the ground to sleep.

During the rest of January we remained in that miserable area, sleeping on the cold, muddy ground. It rained almost every day but was usually clear and cold at night. The tents leaked so our clothing, blankets, and equipment were soon covered with mud and saturated with water.

On 14 January, I was transferred to Company D, 135th Infantry, and had to move across a rocky hill to a new area. My battalion commander was Lt. Col. Robert P. Miller, a former dentist of Appleton, Minnesota. My company commander was 1st Lt. Arnold N. Brandt, a large, good-natured, hardworking officer from Minnesota. The lieutenants assigned to the company were Fotakis, from Boston; Second Lieutenant Bovain, a serious-minded young man; and Second Lieutenant Myers, a young officer who had been an Infantry School instructor. Company D, like Company H, which I had left in October, was the heavy weapons company of the First Battalion and was organized like Company H. Although I had been merely a platoon leader in Company K, in Company D I was the second in command and executive officer.

At that time, an infantry rifle battalion consisted of approximately 870 men organized into three rifle companies each commanded by a captain, one heavy weapons company commanded by a captain, and a battalion headquarters company. An infantry battalion was commanded by a lieutenant colonel, with a major as his second in command. Also included in battalion headquarters were the following special staff officers: an adjutant and S-1 who supervised billeting, morale, and routine reports; an S-2, or intelligence officer, who supervised the collection of information about the enemy; an S-3, or plans, training, and operations officer; an S-4 who was the supply officer charged with procuring food, clothing, and other supplies for the battalion; and a communications officer who was responsible for the supervision and maintenance of all telephones, radios, and messenger services.

The basic assault unit for close combat with the enemy was the rifle company of approximately 185 men. This unit included three rifle platoons, each led by a second lieutenant and one weapons platoon led by a first lieutenant. Each rifle platoon was further subdivided into three squads of twelve men each, each squad in turn commanded by a staff sergeant. These squads and platoons did the major share of bloody close-in fighting with the enemy; hence, the winning of the entire war depended mainly on the tenacity, courage, and skill with which the second lieutenants and staff sergeants directed the platoons and squads under their command.

At the time I joined the First Battalion in 1943, it was commanded by Lt. Col. Robert P. Miller, with Maj. Garnett Hall as executive officer; Capt. Don Landon as CO (commanding officer) of Company A, 1st Lt. John Lyons as executive officer; First Lieutenant Tucker, CO of Company B, First Lieutenant Midkiff as executive officer; Capt. Charles Fanning, CO of Company C, 1st Lt. Frank Openshaw as executive officer; 1st Lt. Arnold N. Brandt as CO of Company D, with me as his executive officer. On the battalion staff were 1st Lt. Maurice Stacy, S-1 and adjutant; 1st Lt. William E. Smith, S-2; Capt. Raymond W. Sellers, S-3; 2d Lt. Anthony Von Ruden, S-4; First Lieutenant Anderson, battalion communications officer. Among the junior officers in the companies at that time were Second Lieutenant Koulgeorge, Second Lieutenant Gould, Lt. Rufus B. O'Farrell, Second Lieutenant Perry, Lieutenant Richardson, Lieutenant Henley, and 1st Lt. Gail R. Bell. Besides these officers, there was Captain Hamblin, the battalion surgeon, and Father Cashman, the battalion chaplain. There were approximately thirty-six officers serving with the First Battalion. Many of these officers were either killed in action, wounded, or captured during the fierce fighting of the First Battalion in Tunisia and Italy. Of the number listed in this paragraph, First Lieutenant Midkiff, Second Lieutenant Von Ruden, Second Lieutenant Koulgeorge, Second Lieutenant Gould, Lieutenant O'Farrell, and First Lieutenant Richardson were killed in action. Lieutenant Colonel Miller, Captain Fanning, First Lieutenant Openshaw, First Lieutenant Lyons, First Lieutenant Tucker, First Lieutenant Anderson, First Lieutenant Smith, First Lieutenant Stacy, and many others not listed were either killed or wounded in action. Second Lieutenant Perry was captured by the Germans.

At a meeting of our battalion officers shortly after I joined it, we were informed that we would remain in our present location not more than six weeks, after which we would engage in the fighting in Tunisia. This meant a hard training schedule with little time for rest or recreation. Weather and ground were both ideally suited to hard training, the former remaining uniformly wet and cold, and the latter being muddy and rocky. We were on a continuous seven-day training schedule. Our only relaxation during this vigorous life was the drinking of delicious wine in the evenings, accompanied by group singing of popular tunes such as "(You'll Be Mine in) Apple Blossom Time."

On 28 January 1943, we were alerted for an immediate move into central Tunisia where the Thirty-fourth Division was to take over a large sector of the front that had been occupied by French troops since November.

We were instructed to familiarize ourselves with rules, regulations, and instructions in our field manuals on procedures for relief of frontline rifle companies.

First Lieutenant Openshaw from Company C, Lieutenant Henley from Company A, First Lieutenant Midkiff from Company B, and I were designated as an advance party to precede the main body of the First Battalion into Tunisia in a large command car to be used for reconnaissance and planning upon our arrival in Tunisia.

Chapter XII
Journey to Tunisia

Early on 29 January 1943, elements of the advance quartering detail assembled at Thirty-fourth Division Headquarters. Transportation for the group consisted of some forty assorted trucks, command cars, and jeeps under command of Lt. Col. Albert Svoboda, commanding officer of the Second Battalion, 135th Infantry.

During our first day of travel, we made excellent time in bright, clear weather. We halted two hours before dark just inside a large racetrack near Sidi-bel-Abbès, the home of the French Foreign Legion. We were not permitted to enter the city lest the secrecy of our journey be compromised. After eating a meal of C rations, we rolled up in our blankets and slept.

The second and third days passed uneventfully as we continued our journey eastward to the outskirts of Algiers, where we halted for our third night in a large field beside the road. I listened to a radio in one of the armored scout cars of our cavalry reconnaissance troops, which, in addition to the announcement that *"Le Huitième Armée Brittanique continue l'attacque en Tunisie,"* conveyed the thrilling news that Gen. Bernard L. Montgomery, in close pursuit of Field Marshal Erwin Rommel, had just crossed the border from Tripolitania into Tunisia. Another part of the radio program was taken up by a spirited plea to the American people to continue the game of baseball. The speaker's principal argument was based on the fact that the boys in the armed forces would be disappointed if baseball in America were allowed to die. His argument concluded with the statement that not only did the fighting men want baseball to continue, but also it would provide needed relaxation and rest for the overworked defense laborers. I was so weary from living in the mud, cold, and rain I did not care if baseball in America were allowed to die and the overworked defense laborers had no recreation.

A sudden air-raid warning from the sirens in Algiers broke up the group listening to the radio, as we heard the hum of many German planes in the sky to our rear. Although none came near us, we saw the brilliant display of streaking antiaircraft fire across the black sky from many directions. The planes were quickly driven off by the fire, and we rolled up once more in our blankets.

On the second day out of Algiers, our route along the Mediterranean coast led us through hilly, barren country. We travelled through this inhospitable region until the afternoon of 2 February when the command car in which Openshaw, Midkiff, Henley, and I were riding developed engine trouble and left us far behind the rest of the convoy.

By the time we completed enough repairs to resume our journey, it was so late we decided to travel all night in our effort to overtake the convoy. We had previously heard rumors that German paratroopers were frequently dropped in this area to disrupt the five-hundred-mile-long American lines of communications leading from Algiers into Tunisia. This caused us to be apprehensive.

The narrow road along which we travelled was often bordered on both sides by deep cuts, high hills, and steep cliffs. This resulted in slow travel. We were forced to turn on our headlights in violation of orders. We thus became an excellent target for any paratroopers or enemy planes that might be in the vicinity. We sat tensely in our seats with rifles loaded and ready for instant use. We tried, without success, to see through the gloomy darkness on either side of the road. At our slow rate of travel, it would have been easy for an enemy paratrooper to toss a hand grenade into our car as it passed close to the steep cuts and banks on both sides of the road.

Suddenly, we heard a loud crack like that of a pistol shot to our immediate rear. While we trembled and grasped our rifles tensely, a large U.S. Army truck suddenly rounded a sharp curve behind us and backfired loudly several more times as the driver slowed down quickly to avoid hitting us.

On the morning of 3 February, we overtook our convoy just as it was pulling out of the bivouac area where the troops had spent the night.

Throughout the day we travelled through the barren country of eastern Algeria. Almost a desert, it was devoid of agriculture, with rocky hills covered with scattered cactus patches, straw huts, ragged Arabs, and flocks of thin goats.

As we neared the Tunisian border, we extended the interval between vehicles in the convoy to more than two hundred yards. We lowered their tops and stationed an observer in each to keep a constant lookout in all directions for enemy planes, which had recently made frequent strafing attacks on convoys in this area.

Each time we halted to brew coffee and eat C rations, a large group of ragged Arab children converged on us. They stared at us like starved dogs begging for scraps.

I finally inquired in French of a sixteen-year-old boy why his people harassed the U.S. soldiers so persistently for food and cigarettes.

"All you Americans are *reech*," he replied. "I am but a poor Arab whom the damn French have robbed and stole from for so long, we got nothing left, therefore you *reech* Americans should give us plenty money."

"I'll be glad to change places with you," I replied. "You take my place and go to Tunisia and get killed by the Germans. I'll put on your clothes and stay here until the war is over."

"No! American soldier you won't get killed," he replied, shaking his head violently, "because you have been kind to the poor Arabs."

We frequently met large groups of people travelling west with their camels, horses, and household goods. Invariably, the men rode proudly astride their camels while their wives trudged wearily on foot behind them.

Lieutenant Openshaw asked an Arab, who had a long white beard and mantle and who bore a striking resemblance to one of the Three Wise Men, to pose for a picture riding a large camel with a little camel following behind. The Arab obligingly posed for the picture, but then demanded that Openshaw pay him for permitting the picture to be taken. Lieutenant Openshaw angrily refused to pay.

On 5 February, we travelled all night over a narrow, muddy road. Our most advanced airfields were so far behind us the Germans controlled the air, making it difficult for our troops and vehicles to move by day. During the day and most of the night, we passed through a mountainous region of cork forests. The ground was covered with snow.

At dawn on 6 February, we entered a wooded area of Macktar Forest in central Tunisia. It was near British First Army Headquarters west of the village of Pichon. We bivouacked under the trees.

Chapter XIII
On the Defensive in Pichon

We spent 6 February digging foxholes. When the foxholes were finished, we rested. The main body of the Thirty-fourth Division (approximately fifteen thousand troops) arrived on 7 February at 2200 hours. We met them and guided the units into the areas that we had selected and laid out for them during daylight.

On 8 February, all 135th Infantry battalion commanders went forward to the front lines to make a reconnaissance with Col. Robert W. Ward, our regimental commander. This was followed on 9 February by the battalion commanders going forward with their company commanders to make a more detailed reconnaissance.

Finally, on 10 February, I went forward, as company executive officer of Company D, with Captain Brandt and the platoon leaders. We rode in a jeep at high speed through rocky, cactus country strewn with the burnt hulks of tanks and jeeps destroyed by German planes. Here and there beside the road, the bloated carcass of a mule lay rigidly on its back, with its feet protruding stiffly toward the sky.

After a few minutes we crossed a little wadi, or dry stream bed, made a sharp right turn and proceeded along a road bordered on its left by a large olive orchard and on the right by a dense thicket of tall cactus. The road led through a broad valley covered with olive trees, cactus, and brush into the shell-scarred town of Pichon. Upon arriving in Pichon, we parked our jeeps among the olive trees and proceeded the rest of the way to the front lines on foot.

A few stone buildings in town were still standing, but most of them had been demolished by enemy artillery shells. Near the center of town the road was intersected by another which led due east about thirty miles to Kairouan, the holy Mohammedan city.

Immediately west of the road intersection stood the only building in town that had not been hit by artillery fire. It stood in a grove of olive and almond trees on a small hill partly concealed by a hedge of cactus. On the second floor of this large stone building was a small balcony that commanded an excellent view of the German positions to the east. It had been used by the French commander in the area as a battalion command and observation post, even though it violated the principles for selecting command and observation posts. The Germans evidently thought that nobody was fool enough to occupy the building, and for that reason they did not choose to waste their fire on it.

When we entered the heavily sandbagged basement of the building, we were pleasantly surprised to meet and to receive a short briefing on the local tactical situation at the front from Brig. Gen. Theodore Roosevelt, Jr., assistant division commander of the First Infantry Division, which occupied frontline positions near those of the French soldiers.

After our unexpected briefing provided by General Roosevelt, one of the bravest and best combat leaders of World War II, we climbed the stairs of the observation post in order to use our field glasses to study the frontline positions as viewed from the second-floor balcony of the building.

On the east side of the road, directly across from the battalion observation post, stood a thick grove of olive trees, beneath which were many deep, well-sandbagged dugouts. They contained an intricate system of underground passages, which had been used by the French headquarters personnel. According to one of the French soldiers, about three weeks previously a German patrol had infiltrated the front lines, entered the olive grove, and tossed a hand grenade into one of the dugouts, killing the French battalion commander and wounding several enlisted men.

About twelve hundred yards east of the command post, a low

ridge covered with high grass, bushes, and scattered olive trees ran parallel to the road through the valley. Along the crest of this ridge, the French had set up their frontline defenses. To the southeast about four or five miles, rising almost straight up through the cold, clear Tunisian air, we could see the barren blue mountain, Djebel Trozzia. Far to the east we saw another rocky ridge, whose steep slopes were white with snow and which undoubtedly gave the Germans a superb view of the entire area that we occupied.

After we left the observation post building and made our way cautiously to the front lines, we split into small groups and concealed ourselves as much as possible behind all available trees and bushes. We passed through the French reserve company, located about six hundred yards behind the front lines on a small hill surrounded by barbed wire. To its front was a marshy area covered by a thick grove of tall eucalyptus trees.

The soldiers in the long frontline positions were strung out thinly. They had been in these positions several weeks. They were well dug in with an intricate system of camouflaged dugouts, winding trenches, and excellent observation posts. They were ragged and poorly armed with World War I rifles and machine guns. They were supported by British artillery and tanks. In this quiet sector, the German lines were about one to five kilometers away.

After we made arrangements to have a guide from each one of the French platoons meet each of our platoons at a previously designated spot on the highway in rear of the front lines, we returned to our jeeps and sped back to Macktar Forest to find that the first sergeants had already got all the companies of the battalion ready to move. We were to take with us to the front lines only our bedding rolls, the clothes on our backs, one extra handkerchief, and an extra pair of socks. Everything else was loaded on trucks and hauled back to Le Kef, several miles west of Macktar Forest.

After a hot meal we proceeded slowly by truck toward the front lines. It was a dark, misty night with thick clouds obscuring the moon and stars. When we finally crossed the bridge over the shallow wadi, some fifteen hundred yards behind the front, it was about 0200 hours. We unloaded from the trucks at this point and walked the rest of the way. Colonel Ward, the regimental commander, stood by the road and personally spoke to each lieutenant as he passed, grasped his hand firmly, and wished him good luck.

It was so dark that we could not see how to get our kitchen and headquarters set up in the olive grove where we had temporarily halted for the night. We, therefore, rolled up in our blankets to await the arrival of dawn. Meanwhile the platoons of Company D went forward into their frontline positions with the rifle platoons they were supporting.

I awoke on the morning of 11 February with the steady drip of a cold rain beating into my face from the branches of the olive tree over my head. After a breakfast of corned beef and hard crackers, I walked toward the front lines to find a location for company headquarters and for the four 81-mm mortars. We decided to leave the kitchen in the olive grove near the road about a thousand yards behind the front, where supplies could be delivered more easily.

Assisted by First Sergeant Zimmerman, I selected for the command post several dugouts constructed by the French soldiers. Each dugout had a log roof covered with dirt, rocks, and iron beams, and a straw-covered floor. Each one was carefully concealed by the branches of an olive tree growing over it. The area had formerly been a beautiful garden with a deep well in its center, surrounded by almond and lemon trees. It was about seven hundred yards behind the frontline rifle company positions.

About two hundred yards in front of the company command post we emplaced the 81-mm mortars in a central position in another garden surrounded by a thick hedge of cactus bushes, which we hoped would effectively conceal the mortars from the observation of German patrols.

Our troops were thinly spread out. Our battalion covered a front of almost three miles instead of the usual one-half mile considered normal for an infantry battalion. It was necessary for me to spend the rest of the day reconnoitering the front lines and studying means of installing telephone communications to the scattered machine-gun and mortar positions across the entire width of the battalion.

Shortly after moving into the front lines, we received orders that our mission was to remain in these positions and fight to the last round of ammunition. Our defense plan called for B Company on the right of the battalion sector, A Company on the left, and C Company in reserve about eight hundred yards to the rear, ready to rush into any breach that might be created by the attacking Germans. Our right flank was the most vulnerable since a paved road led through a gap in the ridge and thence all the way to the city of Kairouan. This road seemed to be an excellent avenue for the approach of hostile tanks into our position. Consequently, it was well covered by mines, artillery concentrations, and antitank guns.

During the first two days and nights, we saw little action except artillery fire and patrol activity. Nobody was killed, but a few men from Company B were slightly wounded. Apparently our front was lightly held by the enemy.

At about 2000 hours on 13 February, an unidentified plane circled low over our battalion sector. I immediately dived into my dugout, prefacing my action by ordering everyone else in the immediate vicinity to do likewise. About three hundred yards north of us, three blinding flashes of light suddenly mushroomed from the ground followed instantly by the thunderous crash of exploding enemy bombs. The bombs scored a direct hit on the command post of Company C, severely wounding Captain Fanning and several others, and instantly killing several enlisted men. It was later rumored that someone had carelessly struck a match and disclosed our positions to the pilot of the plane.

Chapter XIV
Retreat from Pichon

On the night of 14 February we were warned to keep a sharp lookout for enemy paratroopers. When some enemy planes flew low over our area, we suddenly heard the weird cries of a Tunisian bird similar to our American whippoorwill. Immediately each bush and shrub seemed to come alive and quiver in the bright moonlight. As I strained my eyes to see more clearly, I thought I saw the skulking outline of a man dart from behind an olive tree and run into a concealed position behind a low bush. Both Captain Brandt and I grabbed our rifles and dashed madly after the retreating figure, demanding in loud voices for it to halt, but without success. We never learned what it was. It may have been an Arab, a friendly messenger, or a German paratrooper; or it may have been merely a phantasmagoric figment of our overworked imaginations.

The next night was also replete with excitement. We were warned of a possible full-scale enemy attack. We received the usual rumors of enemy tanks moving to our front and paratroopers moving in our rear, but nothing materialized. Throughout the night we could see, far to the south toward the Kasserine and Faïd passes, the orange flashes of continuous artillery fire indicating heavy action.

On the morning of 15 February, the air was charged with intense excitement. We were warned of a possible withdrawal from action on the night of 16 February. Rumors filled the air. Reports of tanks in front of us kept circulating among us. During the morning all company commanders went with the battalion commander for a reconnaissance of the rear area. They did not return until after sundown.

Shortly after the return of the battalion and company commanders, we were alerted for a move to the rear, scheduled to commence at 2000 hours that same day. Shortly after sundown, the enemy laid down a heavy, but scattered, barrage of artillery shells in all parts of our battalion area that miraculously did but little damage. Promptly at dusk, the kitchens of all companies, with all heavy trucks and supplies, started moving to the rear.

At the Company D Command Post, the telephone kept ringing incessantly. Once it was the battalion adjutant calling to inform me that enemy paratroopers had landed in our rear. Again, it was the battalion S-3 warning me that large numbers of tanks were moving toward our lines from the front. Still another time, it was the 2d Machine-Gun Platoon leader informing me that a heavy concentration of enemy mortar fire was falling in his platoon area. On another occasion, the Antitank Platoon leader informed me that a large enemy patrol was infiltrating among his men and firing on them with machine pistols. Meanwhile, the battalion commander, Lieutenant Colonel Miller, called to inform me that it looked like we might have a hard fight to extricate ourselves from our present positions. Meanwhile, the company commander of Company D had been conferring with the battalion commander and had left the running of the company to me.

The night was dark with thick clouds obscuring the moon and stars. A heavy mist cut ground visibility to almost zero. I had previously designated a rendezvous area at a road junction a few hundred yards to the rear where I ordered the platoons of Company D to meet me at a given time. As soon as I received the report from the last platoon leader that he was on his way out, I assembled the personnel of company headquarters and struck out for the road junction with all possible speed. To my dismay, I discovered that the main body of the battalion had already arrived and was now at least one-half mile ahead of us.

Meanwhile, one platoon from Company B remained in position to cover our withdrawal while a battery of the 125th Field Artillery Battalion laid a heavy barrage of shells on the enemy positions to drown out noise and create confusion among the enemy if they tried to attack us.

Although the men were heavily loaded with ammunition, overcoats, and blankets, I ordered them to set a fast rate of march and try to catch up with the other companies as quickly as possible. A steady drizzle was soaking our clothes, increasing their weight and making it difficult for us to march rapidly.

Suddenly the silence was shattered by the staccato crash of several enemy machine guns directly to our rear. This provided such a sudden impetus to all that we were soon swinging down the road rapidly and in perfect cadence. In a few minutes, we overtook the main body and continued to march for another eight miles and then halted. We mounted trucks and rode for the rest of the night over the narrow roads, which the battalion and company commanders had reconnoitered on the preceding day.

At daybreak we arrived in a broad cactus-covered valley near the town of Sbiba. We pitched our pup tents and rested throughout the day.

For several days we were continually on the move, mostly under cover of darkness. On the outskirts of Sbiba we reconnoitered the area and dug foxholes as though planning to stay a long time. However, we spent only one night and one more day in the area and moved out at dusk the next night for several miles, halting under the banks of a broad, deep wadi. I spent the morning reconnoitering several forward routes for the battalion in case we should be ordered to attack the Germans.

The Germans had made an all-out attack through Kasserine Pass, had knifed through our division, and had almost completely destroyed the 168th Infantry Regiment. In the afternoon twilight, we had an excellent view of part of the battle and could see in the distance many American tanks being destroyed and set on fire by the Germans.

Word reached us the next day that the German attack was still rolling forward and that we would probably have to make another withdrawal of five miles the next day. With the company commanders and other company executive officers, I spent most of the afternoon reconnoitering new defensive positions on the far side of a broad wadi that seemed impassable to tanks.

When we returned to the battalion area, our battalion was already in motion to the rear because the Germans had again broken through the American defenders, causing our move to be made twenty-four hours earlier than scheduled.

As we trudged wearily through the darkness, a cold drizzle fell, wetting us to the skin and causing us to slip and slide awkwardly through the sticky mud. We, at length, arrived at our new positions at 0200 hours in such intense darkness that we could do little except dig foxholes and hope that the Germans would also bog down in the sticky mud.

The arrival of a cold, rainy morning shielded us from air observation. We were able to organize our positions rapidly for defense. We saw that we were in the middle of a level, marshy wheat field facing north. To our front was a deep wadi, to our left a range of steep, rocky hills clad with evergreen trees, and to our right a range of barren mountains. Far to our front, many miles away across the flat valley floor, the massive outline of Djebel Trozzia rose majestically to the sky. About a thousand yards to the rear of the front lines, almost in the center of the valley, rose a round hill to a height of about fifty yards. It afforded an excellent battalion observation post because of the view it offered for many miles ahead. Near the hill stood the large house of a prosperous Arab farmer who owned the wheat field and many cattle. Evidently, a large lake had once covered the valley floor, thus creating the unusual condition of making it possible for an Arab to be rich. (This was several years before oil was discovered in North Africa on Arab lands.)

At noon we received word that the Germans had arrived at the positions we occupied the preceding night but had been repulsed by a battalion of the 133d Infantry with the loss of several tanks. The Germans then withdrew through Kasserine Pass under the steady pounding of United States Air Force bombers and fighter planes.

We occupied positions in the wheat field for several days. Throughout the period the Arab farmer, whose land we occupied, deeply resented our presence. He flooded his irrigation ditches in an effort to dislodge us, but we were so inured to water and mud this didn't bother us. During this period, one of our patrols accidentally killed one of the Arab farmer's cows with a stray rifle shot. Our cooks butchered the cow and cooked several juicy steaks and roast beef from the carcass, which tasted delicious after subsisting so long on C and British compote rations. The farmer immediately raised such hell through official channels that we had to pay him the sum of five hundred dollars damages. That was the most expensive beef we had ever eaten. No wonder this Arab was a rich man.

Chapter XV
Routine Patrol Activity

March 1, 1943, was a memorable day for me. On that day I received a cablegram from my wife, Sarah, back in Williamston, North Carolina, stating that a son, Leslie W. Bailey, Jr., had been born to us on January 28, 1943. It had taken the cablegram only thirty-one days to reach me. However, this was typical of the North African Cable Services at that time.

On the night of 1 March, we commenced a slow move forward on foot for ten miles to a low ridge of cactus-covered hills that crossed the entire width of Sbiba Valley. The night was so black we could not see the muddy trail over which we floundered. Rain was falling so rapidly it soon filled the ruts and shell craters in the road to a depth of several inches. We held tightly to each other to avoid falling. However, the mud was so slippery that our forward progress was often interrupted by heavy falls, punctuated by loud curses of exasperation. After each fall, we rose painfully to our feet and proceeded cautiously forward a few steps only to slide, slip, and fall heavily again into the muddy water.

Finally, about two hours before daybreak, we waded up to our waists through the cold water of a flooded stream and reached our new defensive positions. I flopped to the ground, but the chilling wind and the cold night air roused me and caused me to pace back and forth for the remainder of the night.

With the arrival of day, the warm sunshine soon dried our clothes and made life bearable once more. We immediately started a systematic organization of our defensive positions.

For several days, we continued to improve our positions along the crest of the ridge, which crossed the entire length of the valley. Our positions afforded us observation of the valley all the way to Djebel Trozzia several miles away. We dug foxholes deep enough for a man to stand erect and still have enough leeway for a tank to pass directly over his head without harming him. We sited our rifles and machine guns to cover all avenues of enemy approach with grazing fire parallel to the ground and no higher than a man's head. The engineers laid barbed wire entanglements along the front with extensive minefields and booby traps covering likely avenues of enemy approach. The artillery provided us with preplanned barrages to cover critical areas of probable enemy approach. We reconnoitered routes to the rear in case the enemy should attack in overwhelming force, requiring us to fall back all the way to the positions we had just vacated.

The German positions were thought to be several miles ahead of us at Fondouk Pass. We received no artillery fire from them and engaged only in routine patrol activity. We were able to pitch pup tents and sleep in warm blankets every night. Our patrols of ten to twelve men went out nightly to Djebel Trozzia without contacting the Germans. Finally, our Third Battalion went to the vicinity of Pichon where, after a sharp battle with the Germans, it withdrew.

Our Company D Command Post was located in a sandy wadi under two fig trees behind the ridge on which the frontline companies were located. This area was covered with a thick growth of cactus. On one occasion a heavy rain fell and the water rose so fast in the wadi that each of us received a sudden but much needed bath.

Meanwhile, back at Le Kef, the Germans bombed our clothing and supply warehouses and destroyed everything we had stored there. We had to wear rags and tatters for many days thereafter. Food was so scarce we ate but two meals per day. Our fare consisted solely of beans, hash, stew, hard biscuits, and coffee with a little chocolate occasionally. We had no fruit of any kind. We could obtain only three packages of secondary brand cigarettes per week.

We never saw Camel, Lucky Strike, Philip Morris, or Chesterfield cigarettes. We heard rumors that in Oran and Algiers the base section troops could buy two cartons per week of their favorite brand cigarettes and that they had fruit cocktail every day. These rumors engendered bitterness and low morale among us. Large sores appeared on the legs of many of us, making it impossible for those so affected to wear leggings. Some of us acquired cooties, or body lice. Such things as a Rest Camp and a Bath and Clothing Exchange Unit were unheard of.

On 20 March, I was sent back to Clairfontaine (Clear Fountain, in English) in eastern Algeria for a ten-day course of instruction at a British battle school conducted by outstanding British army combat officers from the First Army Coldstream Guards and units of the Eighth Army. Although the instruction was excellent and the daily talks by Gen. Harold Alexander and other famous British leaders were inspiring, most of us appreciated best of all the hot food, wine, hot showers, and dry tents.

School ended on 1 April, but I could not get a truck to carry me back to the 34th Division until 3 April. During the trip back to the front, I spent one night in a stone building with some military police officers in Tebessa. I had slept so long in the open, I had difficulty sleeping inside the house because the air inside of it seemed so stuffy.

When I arrived in the First Battalion area, it had moved to the vicinity of the village of Hajeb El Aoun after the 135th Infantry made an unsuccessful attempt to seize the German positions at Fondouk Pass and cut off Field Marshal Erwin Rommel's forces, which were retreating north after their defeat by British General Montgomery at the Mareth Line. The First Battalion was in regimental reserve during the attack and had suffered no casualties.

The battalion positions were located on a sandy ridge in front of a broad wadi. The enemy lines were five miles east along a series of jagged, rocky hills on both sides of Fondouk Pass. Between us and the Germans lay a flat valley, devoid of any cover except a few scattered bushes. To the left of the pass and closer to us rose the steep, rocky hill of El Rhorab. A narrow paved road extended through the entire length of the valley ahead of us and led through Fondouk Pass and across the plains to Kairouan, thirty miles away.

On 5 April I received orders to report to the battalion commander as the Battalion S-3; plans, training, and operations officer. Although I hated to leave Company D, I was glad to receive the opportunity of performing the duties of such a responsible assignment.

On the morning of 6 April, Lieutenant Colonel Miller was ordered to report to Colonel Ward for important orders. When he returned at noon, he informed us that the entire 135th Infantry Regiment would move forward on the night of 7 April, attack the German positions at Fondouk Pass, and seize the high ground on both sides of the pass.

Chapter XVI
The Battle of Fondouk Pass

The mission of our battalion was to move during the night of 7 April, with the other two battalions of our regiment, and seize the high ground on both sides of Fondouk Pass. This action, if successful, would permit a large British armored unit to move quickly through the pass from the west and seize the escape routes of Field Marshal Erwin Rommel's Afrika Korps, which had been defeated recently by General Montgomery's Eighth British Army. In this battle, the Germans had been driven from their positions on the Mareth Line and were now slowly retreating north along the main road a few miles to the east of Fondouk Pass.

After a day of preparation for the attack, we moved forward on foot shortly after dark on 7 April. Our initial goal was a forward assembly area in a sandy wadi about six miles to the left of our present location. After a short halt in the assembly area, we were supposed to continue our advance to a position on the south of Mount El Rhorab, a steep rocky hill on the left flank of the two assaulting battalions of our regiment.

After much cursing and milling around in the dark for several minutes, we finally got on the right trail and arrived at our initial objective before daylight. While we waited to move forward again, we received word to complete our move after daylight. The remainder of the night was so bitterly cold we suffered intensely.

A few minutes before dawn all hell broke loose as our artillery shells whistled over our heads and crashed in a brilliant shower of sparks among the jagged hills ahead of us. The dim gray outline of the hills assumed a clear shade of blue as the light of dawn streaked the sky. We saw the hills covered with a thick blanket of brownish-yellow explosions. We did not receive a single round of return fire from the Germans.

Our artillery fire continued intermittently until about 0800, when we were informed that the attacks of the Second and Third Battalions had bogged down in the flat valley several hundred yards short of the pass. The First Battalion was then ordered to move immediately across the open ground between us and the enemy in the hills to a position on the right of Mount El Rhorab and then dig in to protect the left flanks of the Second and Third Battalions from the German troops on the mountain.

I have seen the battlefield at Gettysburg, Pennsylvania, where Gen. George Pickett and his men made their futile charge against the strongly entrenched Yankees on Cemetery Hill. At Fondouk Pass our situation was almost identical to that faced by General Pickett at the Battle of Gettysburg. The ground between us and the Germans was flat and offered us no cover or concealment except scattered bushes and tall weeds. The Germans occupied high, rocky hills to our front and on our left flank. Moreover, the clear weather offered them perfect observation of our positions and any movement we might make toward them. I was well aware of the extreme difficulty and danger of our mission. It seemed to me that we were about to reenact a modern version of the famous charge of the British Light Brigade at Balaclava during the Crimean War.

Our battalion commander disposed his forces with intervals of one hundred yards between companies and five yards between men, with two companies abreast of each other in the lead, one slightly to the right rear, and the third company following the left company. As we advanced rapidly, several hundred yards toward the enemy, not a shot was fired at us.

Since I was a battalion staff officer, I marched with Company C, the left rear company of the battalion, in a small group with First Lieutenant Richardson. As we crossed a shallow gulch I suddenly saw several puffs of white smoke burst in rapid succession from the ground at the base of the hills ahead of us. Immediately a loud whistling noise roared through the air over our heads. I looked back just in time to see four enemy shells crash into the sand about four hundred yards to my rear. Again I saw the white smoke puffs followed by the whistle, and this time the shells crashed into the sand only two hundred yards to the rear of our advancing battalion.

As the shells landed closer to us, their whistling increased in volume and intensity. In a few seconds a terrifying barrage of enemy shells was covering the entire length and breadth of our battalion. Meanwhile, we continued to move forward toward the enemy, standing erect like the British Regulars charging up Bunker Hill in the Revolutionary War. On all sides of me our soldiers were being mowed down like grass by the withering blast of flying steel that now rained like hail among us.

Frantically, I tried to remember the advice I had received at the U.S. Army Infantry School on the best action to take when being shelled by enemy artillery. Like my fellow soldiers I moved forward in short rushes at top speed, then flopped to the ground behind any available bush or slight fold in the ground, then got up and reluctantly ran forward again. The soft sand made running difficult, particularly since I carried a heavy combat pack, a map case, field glasses, six cans of C rations and a ten-pound rifle.

Suddenly, I heard a whistling roar like a freight train coming directly toward me. I flung myself against the ground just as two tremendous explosions hit the ground near me, one a few feet to my left front and the other about fifteen feet to my right rear. The blast from the first explosions lifted my helmet from my head as shrapnel whined past my ears. I clamped my helmet tightly on my head just as the second shell hit the ground, covering me with dirt, filling my mouth with sand, and leaving me temporarily stunned.

Although I was not hit, my nostrils smarted from the acrid fumes of the burned cordite powder from the exploded shells. Also, a large jagged hole had been torn in the wooden stock of my rifle, which was slung from my shoulder with a leather sling. I realized that only a miracle had saved me from a sudden violent death.

During the brief lull that followed the heavy enemy artillery barrage, I raised my head to see what damage had been done. On all sides of me men were lying in grotesque positions, some covered with blood, some dead, and some badly wounded. A few feet ahead of me, a young lieutenant lay on the ground, groaning and writhing in agony. A medical aid man quickly ripped off the lieutenant's shirt, revealing a tiny wound on the left side of his chest just beneath his collar bone. Blood oozed from the wound in a thin scarlet trickle. Although his wound appeared to be slight, the lieutenant groaned as though he suffered excruciating pain.

Suddenly, another enemy artillery barrage crashed with a thunderous roar into the center of our positions.

When the enemy shelling finally stopped, the medical aid man again crawled up to the wounded lieutenant and carefully checked his pulse. Meanwhile, his face had turned a pasty, bluish white. He was dead. Apparently a small piece of shrapnel had penetrated his heart.

After a few minutes delay, we moved forward through a shallow ditch that led toward our objective, but allowed us to be concealed from the view of the Germans as long as we crawled on our hands and knees.

We crawled on our hands and knees.

We proceeded cautiously until we suddenly encountered a dead German soldier sprawled in the middle of the ditch with his eyes open. A gold tooth gleamed from his open mouth. He wore gray woolen clothing and was extremely emaciated. Although there was a Luger pistol in the holster strapped to his side, nobody dared touch it, because a wire attached to his pistol extended into the bushes beside the ditch. We suspected that the wire was attached to a booby trap, concealed in the bushes, in such a manner that anyone touching the wire would cause the booby trap to detonate and kill him.

The enemy shelling had destroyed our wire communication with our supporting artillery, which greatly increased their difficulty in firing quickly and accurately on the enemy positions. When we arrived at our objective about twelve hundred yards short of the enemy positions and stopped, the shelling abruptly stopped, indicating that the Germans might be short of ammunition.

We took advantage of this unexpected lull in the battle to dig foxholes. In the late afternoon a large number of tanks from the British Sixth Armored Division rolled among our foxholes and halted. This action caused a heavy barrage from the Germans, which the tanks returned. The tanks then rolled forward but were soon stopped by an antitank minefield.

During this action a thin haze of smoke settled over the battlefield, partially shielding us from observation by the Germans. At this time I was fascinated by the demeanor of the British soldiers, who, disregarding the flying shrapnel, calmly crawled out of their tanks, brewed tea, and advised "our lads" to "never mind the 88s. They cawn't hurt you, you know, if you don't get frightened."

During the afternoon we received orders to move forward and seize the high ground on the right of Fondouk Pass. In a few minutes of intense enemy shelling, I sat in a foxhole with the first sergeant of Company C and smoked an entire pack of cigarettes.

As we moved forward again from the safety of our foxholes, the red afternoon sun hung low over Djebel Trozzia and I wondered if I would live long enough to see it rise again the next morning. Meanwhile the Germans continued to shell us, but with reduced effectiveness because of the haze.

We advanced until we were stopped by a fusillade of German mortar, machine-gun, and rifle fire.

As the battalion S-3 I had no command function, but the battalion commander told me to accompany C Company in its attack. When we halted, I crawled into some narrow, winding trenches formerly occupied by the Germans but was so tired I dozed off to sleep.

Later, I awoke to find that I had been asleep for three hours. Nobody was near me. Peering toward the sky I saw a thin cloud, which diffused the moonbeams into a weird half-light that caused nearby objects to assume grotesque shapes.

I raised my head, peered cautiously in all directions, then scrambled to my feet and started walking forward. I assumed that the remainder of the battalion had pulled out toward the objective and left me behind.

When I heard the crackle of several bullets whizzing over my head, I flopped back into my foxhole. With trembling fingers I attempted to pull back the bolt of my rifle and shove a shell into the chamber, but the cartridge magazine was clogged with dirt and sand. It was impossible for me to fire my rifle.

I felt helpless. I began to fancy myself bayoneted from the rear or mutilated by a hand grenade tossed by an infiltrating German patrol. To my right a small clump of bushes seemed to move toward me, each bush wearing the fierce mien of a charging infantryman of the Afrika Korps.

As I lay trembling in the cold sweat which covered me, I distinctly heard the sound of footsteps approaching, mingled with the rattle of canteen cups and the unmistakable cursing of tired American infantrymen. It was a machine-gun platoon of Company D under the command of Lieutenant Fotakis. He told me the remainder of the battalion had withdrawn four hundred yards to the rear. He was on his way to rejoin them. I decided to go with him.

We continued walking in the darkness as silently as possible toward the large steel transmission tower where we hoped to contact our frontline units. Suddenly we thought we heard the challenge, "Halt! Who is there?" We hit the dirt and lay flat on the ground. I yelled out, "Friends," but received no answer. After a diligent search, we found neither friend nor foe anywhere in the vicinity.

Not wishing to wander aimlessly all night, we halted in some abandoned enemy trenches, which we organized into a perimeter defense. We set up four machine guns facing outward in a circle and posted sentries in shifts to give the alarm in case of attack. Although it was bitterly cold, we slept soundly until the roar of incoming enemy artillery shells awakened us just after daylight.

During the night friendly tanks had pulled up on all sides of us and were blasting away at the Germans, who unhesitatingly blasted back at us. Many of the enemy mortar and artillery shells were hitting close, but the trenches in which we lay protected us from the flying shell fragments.

The sun shown brilliantly from a cloudless sky, affording an excellent view of the battlefield. From our position on the left flank of the battalion, we could see across a broad wadi. About four hundred yards to our left flank, a fierce battle was raging between the British and the Germans. The Germans were well entrenched in a village at the base of El Rhorab among cactus bushes and mud huts. Although the German rifle and machine-gun fire was mowing down the British soldiers like ripe wheat under the blade of a keen sickle, the Tommies kept surging forward until they overwhelmed the Germans. With a final bloodcurdling yell, the British soldiers swarmed in among the Germans and wrested their positions from them. Among their booty was five of the German artillery pieces that had wreaked such devastating destruction among us throughout the preceding day.

Throughout the morning enemy artillery fire rained about us with such intensity that we were unable to move from our foxholes. Finally at 1100 hours during a lull in the shelling, we started forward to rejoin the battalion in the attack. Since El Rhorab was now in British hands, we moved in single file under the steep bank of the wadi to the left of the battalion. We proceeded forward for about five hundred yards until the wadi veered off sharply to the left and it was necessary for us to move in the open once more.

Five of us crawled into the open and started to walk in full view of the enemy who instantly unleashed a barrage of mortar and 88-mm shells at us. We dashed forward and executed a simultaneous dive into some unoccupied trenches just in time to avoid being cut to pieces by the hail of shrapnel from the bursting German shells.

The trenches were so deep that the top of the ground was two feet over my head when I stood erect. Evidently the Germans thought the little mound of ground in which the trenches were located was one of our artillery observation posts, because they continued to pound away at us with a heavy concentration of shells. Several of the shells landed within a few feet of the edge of the trench above our heads, scattering sand and dirt into our eyes. Eventually the shelling ceased. Not a man had been scratched.

As we got ready to move forward again, several Stuka dive-bombers appeared in the sky and dropped several heavy bombs in the midst of our troops about two hundred yards to my right.

I decided that since it was late in the afternoon we would wait until dark before attempting again to rejoin the battalion. When darkness fell we moved to our right rear and finally made contact with troops of Company C, who were busily digging foxholes as part of the defensive position of the First Battalion.

As quickly as possible I reported to Lieutenant Colonel Miller. He was both surprised and shocked to see me still alive, since he had neither seen nor heard from me for more than thirty-six hours and had received a report that I had been killed in action, along with Lieutenant Richardson from C Company and several enlisted men, by the heavy artillery fire that hit the company so hard the preceding day.

At 2000 hours on 9 April, we received word from regimental headquarters that Company C would make a midnight attack on the German positions. A few minutes later, the attack order was rescinded. Instead, we were directed to have the entire First Battalion attack at dawn the next day.

It was a cold night, but we slept soundly without receiving any shells or small arms fire from the enemy. At 0500 on 10 April we awakened and prepared to attack.

I accompanied the battalion commander to his observation

post among the enemy trenches, which I had occupied the day before. We had an excellent view of the entire zone of action. Following the usual artillery preparation, our men swarmed onto the high ground to the front, meeting but slight opposition, but enough to cause the death of Lt. Rufus B. O'Farrell, who had already won the Distinguished Service Cross for single-handedly defeating a twenty-man German patrol. In a last courageous assault, he again won the Distinguished Service Cross.

As we moved toward the high ground near Fondouk Pass, it was readily apparent why we had encountered so much difficulty. Instead of occupying the hills, the Germans were deeply entrenched on the flat ground at the base of the high ground. Their machine and antitank guns were so placed that they could cover every square inch of the ground ahead of them with grazing fire. Most of our artillery shells were fired into the hills, thus passing harmlessly over the heads of the entrenched Germans, leaving them ready to spring from their foxholes and mow us down as we advanced.

I endeavored to stay in the tank tracks to avoid stepping on the antipersonnel and antitank mines that the Germans had laid in wide bands across the front of their positions.

As I passed through a small field of ripening wheat, I stopped briefly to stare at two young (I estimated each one to be about nineteen or twenty years old) German soldiers sprawled on the ground beside their machine guns. They wore heavy gray over-coats. Each had a large blanket roll strapped to his back as though set for immediate flight when death struck him down. Their eyes were tightly closed and their faces were as smooth and white as marble statues. It was difficult for me not to feel a surge of admiration for them since they had died so bravely, faithful even unto death, as the hundreds of empty machine-gun cartridge shells beside them so mutely testified.

We proceeded on past the rocky hill where the German artillery observation posts were located and thence over level ground covered by an olive orchard until we arrived on a ridge about a thousand yards to the rear of the main enemy defensive positions.

The flat ground between the two ridges was covered with shell craters scattered in an irregular pattern on both sides of the road leading through the pass. It was here that the Germans had placed most of their indirect fire weapons. I saw a German artilleryman lying near a large shell crater beside his 88-mm gun. He clutched an entrenching shovel tightly in his hand. Its handle had been broken by his frantic efforts to dig a foxhole in the rocky soil beside his gun. At the crucial moment, an American artillery shell had hit so close to him that he had died almost instantly.

As we looked at the ground occupied by the Germans, it was evident that if we had marched up the mountains to the right of them, we could have attacked their artillery positions from the rear and thus achieved surprise, which would have resulted in less casualties for us than those we suffered in the direct assault that we had made.

Meanwhile, tanks of the British Sixth Armored Division were rushed through Fondouk Pass, down the broad highway leading across the plains toward Kairouan, in pursuit of the German army that was now retreating rapidly to the north. Since there was now no need to guard the pass, we moved to the west several hundred yards and pitched our pup tents. While in the rest area, it was necessary to send a detail of soldiers to gather the dead and wounded from the battlefield to prevent Arabs from stealing their clothing and shoes. This resulted in several soldiers, including Chaplain Bell, being killed by antipersonnel mines. There were many Bouncing Betty mines in the area, which jumped into the air when stepped on, detonated, and sent about three hundred steel pellets whistling through the air in all directions at high velocities. Many of our bravest soldiers were killed or severely wounded by these diabolical weapons.

The Sunday after the battle of Fondouk Pass, our battalion chaplain held a special Thanksgiving Service. Attendance was almost 100 percent. Evidently there were not many atheists among us.

Chapter XVII
Rehearsal for the Next Battle

Prior to the battle of Fondouk Pass, we had been on the front lines, living without shelter in rain and mud for more than sixty days. During this time we were seldom out of range of enemy artillery fire. We received little sleep and no rest. We had little opportunity to take a bath or change clothes or eat a decent meal. Our food consisted of C rations, without fruit: namely, hash, coffee, and hard biscuits for breakfast; meat and beans, hard biscuits, and coffee for dinner; and meat and vegetable stew, hard biscuits, and coffee for supper. Only three packages of secondary brand cigarettes per man were available each week.

Another factor that made us unhappy was the rumor concerning rest camps, provided by the British army for its combat men who were sent periodically to the rear for rest, food, clean clothing, and a bath.

There was but little rest for the Thirty-fourth Infantry Division. We moved to the middle of a dusty area in Macktar Forest far from any towns except for the Arab villages of mud huts in the cactus patches. An Arab charged First Lieutenant Dodge ten dollars for a dozen eggs. However, when one hasn't tasted a fresh egg for more than a year, he is not too choosy about price.

During the three-day battle of Fondouk Pass, the Thirty-fourth Infantry Division, of which our battalion was a part, had been temporarily detached from its parent unit, the Second U.S. Army Corps commanded by Maj. Gen. George S. Patton, Jr., and had been attached to a British army corps commanded by Lt. Gen. John Crocker.

After the battle, Crocker, in his blunt remarks to some news correspondents, severely criticized the American junior officers (second lieutenants, first lieutenants, and captains) of the Thirty-fourth Division for their failure to capture Fondouk Pass during the frontal attack he had ordered us to make. It was reported that he stated that the U.S. Thirty-fourth Division should be withdrawn from combat and trained somewhere in the rear area by British officers for further combat.

As a result of Crocker's comments, a feature article appeared in *Time Magazine* concerning our failure to capture Fondouk Pass.

In my opinion, Crocker's criticism of our junior officers was unjust. Our junior officers and enlisted men had shown gallantry, courage, and determination throughout the attack. We made some mistakes, and those of us still alive learned many valuable lessons. One bitter lesson we learned was that a straight frontal attack will seldom succeed if it is launched over open ground against strongly defended positions of a determined enemy, even if the attackers *are* gallant, courageous, and skillful.

This same bitter lesson had been learned by the brave British soldiers who were ordered by their commander, Gen. Sir Edward Packenham to attack Gen. Andrew Jackson's American army behind their cotton bales at the battle of New Orleans on January 8, 1815. It had also been learned by the gallant British junior officers and men of the Light Brigade in their famous cavalry charge in a frontal attack across open ground against the Russian army at Balaclava in the Crimean War in 1854.

However, whether or not the criticism of our conduct during the battle of Fondouk Pass was justified, one fact remained above all others: We failed to capture our objective. Since the world so often judges people only by the result they achieve, one's good intentions are useful only in paving the road to *hell*. After the battle, we plunged into a vigorous schedule of training. We had no time for self-pity or past regret. We worked seven days a week and didn't know when Sunday came. Our training consisted of long hikes, rehearsals of battalion attacks, rehearsals with live ammunition, and training in the tactics of night attacks.

The training program ended abruptly on 23 April. The battalion commander ordered me to take a noncommissioned officer from each company on an advance billeting party to the Sidi Nsir Station near Béja. We proceeded north to the Mediterranean Sea and bivouacked in a cork forest near the city of Tabarka. Soon we received word that our plans were changed and the regiment would not move to that area. We turned southeast instead and rode through fields of green wheat, which extended for miles on both sides of the road.

After passing through Béja, we saw evidence of violent combat. Bomb craters and the rusting hulks of German Tiger tanks littered the roadside. Here and there white wooden crosses indicated where German tank crews were buried beside the road.

We selected an area for our battalion bivouac area in a large wheat field near the railway line, which ran through the valley past Sidi Nsir Station. While I was trying to get the area properly allotted to each company, the wind changed direction and carried to my nostrils the horrible odor of rotting flesh. Upon investigation, I discovered about thirty long-horned cattle lying dead around a stone house whose roof had been blown off by artillery fire. The cattle, which were killed by the artillery fire, had been dead for at least a week. They were covered by huge swarms of gnats and green flies. The atmosphere reeked with such a foul odor it almost produced unconsciousness.

After moving as far away as possible from the dead cattle, we selected another area and lay down on the ground to sleep. The battalion arrived at 2200 hours and the companies moved into their allotted areas without incident.

Early on the following morning I went with the battalion commander in his jeep to make a reconnaissance for the attack on a large hill designated on the map as Djebel Tahent. After travelling for several miles to the east over a narrow, winding dirt road, we arrived at the top of a steep ridge covered with rocks.

From our position on top of the high rocky ridge to the northeast of Sidi Nsir Station, we had an excellent view of the steep, jagged hills and valleys to the north, over which towered a large square-topped hill with steep perpendicular cliffs on its southern and eastern slopes. Although it was more than four miles away, it was such a clear day that the details of the massive hill stood out in bold relief against the blue of the cloudless sky. Around its base we could see a cluster of mud-walled thatched-roof Arab huts and some olive trees. The ground on the right slopes of the hill was gentle and rolling. It was covered with a large field of wheat, full grown, just beginning to turn yellow. Near the top of the hill, the ground rose sharply into sheer cliffs that culminated in a flat, barren top devoid of vegetation except for scraggly grass and some scattered olive trees. Between our position and the large hill, three smaller hills with barren slopes strewn with huge boulders towered skyward. To the left of the main hill mass, another hill rose almost as high and merged into a barren, rocky ridge connecting it with the large hill.

My map indicated that the large hill mass was called Djebel Tahent (Mount Tahent) and its top was 609 meters (approximately 1,998 feet) above sea level. Because of its height in meters, the hill was called Hill 609.

While we were discussing plans to attack Hill 609, a German deserter was brought in to talk to us by soldiers of our sister regiment, the 168th Infantry. He stated in reasonably good English that the hill was only lightly held by a few battle-weary Germans of questionable loyalty and that we could easily capture it by launching an immediate attack with only a single platoon of forty or fifty men.

Whether the story told by the German deserter was fact or merely another diabolical ruse of a clever enemy skillfully devised to cause us to go out on a limb by attacking impetuously, we never found out. In any case it engendered a great deal of excitement and speculation among us as to what course of action we ought to pursue.

After a lively discussion participated in by the battalion commander, the company commanders, several of our battalion staff officers and me, Lieutenant Colonel Miller, the battalion commander, decided that "discretion is the better part of valor." Acting on this wise decision, we immediately returned to our battalion area to consider further the actions we should take to attack Hill 609: the kind of plan to adopt, the time of the attack, and the size of the units.

Chapter XVIII
The Battle of Hill 609

Our plans in the First Battalion, 135th Infantry, for attacking the Germans occupying Hill 609 were a small but vitally important part of the overall plan of the combined British, French, and American forces in Tunisia for destroying or capturing all of the German and Italian armed forces in North Africa.

In April 1943, the Allied ground combat forces in Tunisia numbered more than three hundred thousand officers and men, under the overall command of Gen. Dwight D. Eisenhower (with British Gen. Harold Alexander as his deputy commander).

This large Allied force was opposed all along the Tunisian front by approximately three hundred thousand German and Italian soldiers commanded by the German General von Arnim, the successor of Field Marshal Erwin Rommel, who had recently been recalled by Adolf Hitler, from North Africa to Germany, to help prepare to defend the western front in case the Allied forces should invade France across the English Channel.

The Allied forces in Tunisia consisted of the British Eighth Army, the British First Army, the *Corps Franc D'Afrique* (French Army Corps), and the Second Corps U.S. Army.

The U.S. Second Corps, now commanded by Lt. Gen. Omar N. Bradley (who had succeeded Major General Patton on 15 April), consisted of the First, Ninth, and Thirty-fourth Infantry Divisions, and the First Armored Division.

Our Thirty-fourth Infantry Division at this time was commanded by Maj. Gen. Charles W. Ryder, one of the bravest and most distinguished officers in the United States Army. As an infantry battalion commander, he had won the Distinguished Service Cross in France during World War I. From 1937 to 1941 he performed the exacting duties of Commandant of Cadets at the United States Military Academy, West Point, New York. Within the Thirty-fourth division, he was held in high esteem as a gentleman and a first-rate combat soldier.

We also held our corps commander, Lieutenant General Bradley, in high esteem. He had served under Major General Ryder at West Point as one of his battalion commanders. Later during 1940 and 1941, he had served as Assistant Commandant of the Infantry School, Fort Benning, Georgia. Finally, he had come to North Africa after the Allied landings in November 1942 and had served successively as General Eisenhower's deputy, and later as Major General Patton's deputy during the few weeks that the latter had commanded Second Corps.

Our division plan of attack provided for movement north by the 135th Infantry along a zone two thousand yards wide, with Hill 609 on the extreme right of the Thirty-fourth division zone of action. The 168th Infantry was to occupy the rocky ridge to the left and southwest of Hill 609 to protect the flank of the 135th, while the 133d Infantry would remain in division reserve. The Ninth Infantry Division on our left was separated from us by a gap several miles in width. This gap was covered by mobile reconnaissance cavalry units to quickly inform us of any enemy movement into the gap. There was no gap between us and the First Infantry Division on our right flank.

The 135th Infantry regimental plan of attack provided that the First Battalion would be on the right, the Third Battalion on the left, with Second Battalion in reserve. Troops were to move forward under cover of darkness and, in a furious night assault, move forward rapidly, continuing the attack in a northeasterly direction.

Lieutenant Colonel Miller immediately issued his attack order to the company commanders of the First Battalion. Company A, commanded by Captain Landon would immediately move forward and secure the line of departure before dark, and if possible then move under cover of darkness and capture Hill 609, meanwhile laying a continuous length of white engineer tape behind it to guide the other companies of the battalion to the objective. Company B was to move in column initially behind Company A, then swing to its left onto Hill 609, with Company C in reserve. Company B was commanded by First Lieutenant Tucker, Company C, by Captain Fanning.

Lieutenant Colonel Miller sent me to contact the S-3 of the adjacent Battalion of the First Division on our right. After stumbling in the pitch darkness for about two hours, I finally located the adjacent Battalion S-3 and tried to persuade him that Hill 609 was in his battalion's sector and therefore it should be captured by the First Division. I failed to convince him and returned to my own battalion.

It was a damp, cloudy, cold night of extreme darkness. However, despite these difficulties Company A, led by Captain Landon, moved boldly forward until finally halted by heavy mortar and artillery fire. The men dug foxholes and awaited the arrival of Company B.

On the next day, 29 April, both Companies A and B managed to cross the east–west road to the south of Hill 609 and both dug in on the rocky southern slopes of Hill 529. Shortly after dark on 29 April, Company C launched a night attack, but it met such stiff opposition from the entrenched Germans that it soon bogged down. The Germans were on the northern slopes of Hill 520, just barely beyond the crest of the hill.

Meanwhile, on our left flank the Third Battalion attacked and seized some high ground. The Germans immediately counterattacked behind a heavy barrage of airburst artillery shells but were repulsed by our Third Battalion which doggedly held on to its hard-won position among the rocks.

During the battle of Hill 609, my duties as battalion S-3 (plans, training, and operations staff officer) did not require me to be in any specific location. However, when not otherwise engaged, I remained at the battalion forward observation post. This installation was centrally located on the crest of a hill, just behind the front lines, where the actions of the attacking companies and of the enemy could be continuously observed during daylight. My duties required me to keep in close contact with the battalion commander at all times and to visit each company frequently.

Besides the observation post, another important battalion installation was the battalion command post, which was situated in a large ravine about one mile directly to the rear of the center of the frontline companies. Its position at the base of a large hill provided concealment from direct observation by the Germans and protection from their direct-fire weapons (rifles, machine, and antitank guns). Also, it was the most forward position to which a jeep or truck could deliver food, supplies, and ammunition during daylight. Movement forward beyond the battalion command post had to be made cautiously on foot.

On the morning of the third day of the battle, Lieutenant Colonel Miller directed me to go to the battalion command post to meet two British staff officers from Gen. Bernard L. Montgomery's Eighth Army Headquarters and guide them forward to our battalion observation post, so they could get a firsthand view of what was happening on a critically important battlefront in the American zone of action.

Since it was broad daylight, I wasn't happy about moving to the rear and back again over ground, much of which was under direct observation of the enemy. However, I immediately started moving rapidly but cautiously to the rear, taking advantage of whatever cover and concealment was available—rocks, shadows of hills, cactus clumps, folds in the ground, etc.—and soon arrived at my destination.

The two British officers, a major and a captain, were impeccably dressed in their finest uniforms. Both looked as if they had just stepped off the campus of the Royal Military College at Sandhurst, England. Both had short military haircuts and neatly clipped mustaches. By contrast I had a three-day's growth of beard, my uniform was covered with dust, my combat boots were muddy, and I might easily have been mistaken for a hobo instead of a combat first lieutenant of infantry in the U.S. Army.

The British officers seemed glad to see me. They were polite and courteous and anxious to move forward to the front lines. I cautioned them to move rapidly over ground observed by the enemy; I warned them not to group too closely together as we walked and to take advantage of all available cover and conceal-ment. They accepted my advice, politely, but without comment.

We had travelled but a short distance when I suddenly heard the unmistakable whine of two or three incoming enemy artillery shells that sounded like they might hit close to us. I immediately dived among some rocks beside our path and lay flat on the ground for a few seconds, while the shells crashed with a thunderous roar in a small ravine about fifty yards down the hill to our right rear.

As I arose shamefacedly to my feet, I noticed that the major and the captain were smiling broadly, but neither of them said a word. Neither one of them had taken any evasive action to avoid the incoming enemy shells.

Neither one of them spoke as we continued our journey.

Finally, I remarked, "I certainly do admire your courage, and the calm, cool manner in which you both reacted when those two shells hit so close to us. When enemy shells are hitting close to me, I immediately lie flat on the ground, get behind a tree, or get into the closest available ditch whenever I can and as fast as I can."

To this comment the British major replied, "We are just as much afraid of artillery fire as you are, but we cawn't ever afford to set a bad example to the enlisted men, you know; we cawn't let them know we're frightened of anything. It would ruin their morale if we did."

During the remainder of our trip, I had but little more to say and was glad to leave them with Lieutenant Colonel Miller and excuse myself as quickly as I could.

Meanwhile the tactical action of the attacking companies of the battalion continued unabated.

On 30 April, the First Battalion made a coordinated attack on Hill 531, with Companies A and B abreast of each other. This attack made little progress. During that same night, Companies A and B resumed their furious attack but again failed to capture their objectives. Finally, on 1 May, Companies A and C launched another terrific attack behind a heavy artillery barrage. Following the barrage very closely, Company A managed, after a bitter hand-to-hand potato masher grenade battle near the crest of Hill 531, to get one platoon on the summit of the hill. On the other hand, Company C was stopped cold halfway up the hill and had to dig in with difficulty on its rocky slopes.

On the night of 1 May, Company B reinforced Company C in trying to gain the crest of Hill 531. With this added help, Company C attained its objective by dawn on 2 May. Company B then advanced to the right of and beyond Hill 531 and seized some Roman ruins, which lay on flat ground between the positions of Company C and Hill 609.

Meanwhile, the Second Battalion after a desperate battle during which its commander, Lt. Col. Albert Svoboda, led his troops with such gallantry and bravery that he was awarded the Distinguished Service Cross, managed to get one company on the summit of Hill 609. Concurrently with this action, the Third Battalion managed to get its Company L among the olive trees in the Arab village at the base of Hill 609.

The eastern slopes of Hill 609 were still strongly held by the enemy. Throughout the day on 2 May, they lobbed many mortar and artillery shells among us. From his observation post on Hill 531, Lieutenant Colonel Miller, battalion commander of the First Battalion, suddenly saw approximately 2,500 Germans moving on trucks toward our positions, evidently for a heavy counterattack against us. He personally directed heavy artillery fire on the Germans until their formation was broken up and they were forced to flee to the rear. For this heroic achievement, Lieutenant Colonel Miller was awarded the Silver Star. He was also awarded the Purple Heart Medal because of a slight wound caused by a small piece of shrapnel that passed through his helmet and penetrated his neck.

During the afternoon, Company A moved up to the base of Hill 609 and reinforced Company L. For five days the 135th Infantry had been engaged in a desperate battle with large numbers of Germans of the Barenthin Mountain Regiment, who were firmly entrenched on the dominating ground in the area. A large part of this attack was made by the First Battalion's straight frontal attack against superior numbers of enemy. Finally, however, the pressure of the enemy resistance gradually lessened as the 133d Infantry made a wide flanking movement to the rear of the Germans, causing them to withdraw.

During the night of 2 May, the American First Armored Division passed through our positions and pursued the Germans in their flight to the northeast toward Tunis.

On 3 May, we rested on the slopes of Hill 531 among the German bodies, which littered the hillside. They were lying in a medley of grotesque positions. Their flesh had turned black and was deteriorating rapidly under the action of the hot sun.

One German with long, shaggy hair lay in a half-sitting posture wit his rifle propped crazily against a large boulder. A rifle bullet had struck him squarely in the forehead directly between his eyes and drilled a neat hole clean through his head, taking out a large jagged chunk of his skull from the back of his head and sped on its way. He had died instantly.

A second German soldier lay sprawled among the jagged rocks with his face turned to the sky, his facial muscles horribly contorted. His rifle lay on the ground just beyond his reach. About two feet from him was a small crater, evidently caused by a bursting 60-mm mortar shell, which had severely mangled his legs.

A third German with a youthful face lay in a crawling position with a rifle in his right hand and his field glasses slung round his neck. His blackened face was bloated far beyond its natural size.

Still a fourth German lay flat on the ground with one of his feet blown off by the explosion of a mortar shell.

These four were typical of all the dead on the hillside.

The ground was so rocky that it was impossible for the Germans to dig foxholes to escape the mortar and artillery fire. They had tried to build rock shelters, but the American attack drove forward so swiftly and relentlessly that the Germans were overwhelmed.

Usually our Quartermaster Graves Registration troops are prompt in burying the enemy dead, but in this case they must have been unable to locate the dead Germans. About four weeks after the battle, I revisited the battlefield and was surprised to see the Germans still unburied. Their hair had fallen out and their flesh had deteriorated completely, leaving only grinning skeletons. Meanwhile, the Arabs had stolen their shoes, socks, and whatever else could be looted from the bodies. I promptly reported the location of the enemy dead to higher headquarters.

Hill 609 was the key to the German defenses in Tunisia. After its fall, the Allied forces swept forward on a broad front in pursuit of the retreating Germans.

While this was taking place, we were able to get a few days' rest while the 168th Infantry continued attacking the Germans. At this time we were delighted to read the telegram that General Eisenhower sent to Major General Ryder expressing his pride in Major General Ryder and his splendid division.

After the battle we moved into a large wheat field in a wide valley several miles east of Hill 609. We were so thoroughly exhausted, we slept for an entire day.

Chapter XIX
Victory at Last—in North Africa

From our bivouac area in the valley, we saw the bursting shells of the battle taking place several miles away. The Germans were still fighting a bitter rearguard action. The First Battalion, 135th Infantry, was in division reserve while the 168th Infantry was attacking the Germans in the village of Eddekehila. The Second and Third Battalions of the 135th were moving parallel to the 168th Infantry as it attacked, protecting its right flank.

During the first night in the new area, Lieutenant Colonel Miller sent Captain Brandt and me on a mission across a mountain to reconnoiter a stream crossing, five miles to the northeast. Our mission was to discover if troops and vehicles could make a crossing. We took a jeep to the top of the mountain where the trail ended abruptly. We proceeded the rest of the way on foot.

It was a cold, clear, moonless night with brilliant stars that provided insufficient light to guide our footsteps. We stumbled noisily along, dislodging several stones, until at length we arrived at the bottom of the far side of the mountain, almost exhausted.

We were so tired we didn't particularly care whether we got shot or not. A few hundred yards across the valley on the far side of the river, we noted numerous flares, probably fired into the air by nervous German troops, now badly outnumbered and in full retreat. Captain Brandt got out his flashlight and rashly shone it on his map. Nothing happened, so we took off again through the thick underbrush. We crossed a dirt road and passed through some tall grass and cattails. We could hear innumerable frogs croaking mournfully in the swampy ground to the east. (The valley ran generally in a north–south direction.) We soon arrived at the edge of a sluggish stream with marshy banks thickly overgrown with tall grass and underbrush. Captain Brandt beamed his flashlight into the brush, but we could see nothing but thick grass and underbrush. Suddenly, I lost my footing and splashed into the cold, muddy water up to my neck. I immediately decided the stream was not fordable.

Shortly thereafter we heard somebody creeping toward us through the underbrush. Grasping our carbines firmly, we fell flat on our stomachs and yelled the password. In reply we heard the familiar voice of 1st Lt. Maurice Stacy, assistant regimental S-3. He told us he had just found a route around the mountain to the north that led to a suitable ford in the stream, which was the Medjerda River.

We returned to our bivouac area and gave this information to Lieutenant Colonel Miller. He stated that the information was no longer needed since our plans had been changed by higher head-quarters. I was so tired I barely managed to drag myself to my pup tent where I flopped on the ground and slept soundly until daylight, two hours later.

At noon I was sent forward with a billeting party to reconnoiter a new assembly area about eight miles north of us.

The new First Battalion assembly area was near the south entrance of the broad valley known as the Mousetrap, because it was nearly surrounded by a circle of olive tree-covered hills. A broad, well-paved highway ran straight through the middle of the valley and forked near the north end, the east branch leading through Chouigui (Chewey Gooey) Pass to the town of Tébourba and the west fork to the town of Ferryville and the city of Bizerte.

For several months the Germans concealed antitank guns and heavy artillery pieces among the olive trees in the hills around the perimeter of the valley. Every time Allied troops or tanks tried to enter the Mousetrap through the south entrance, the Germans let them proceed unmolested for several hundred yards, then opened fire on them with heavy artillery and antitank guns.

At the time of our arrival in our new battalion assembly area, I was not fully aware of the extreme danger of taking a single jeep into the Mousetrap. I knew that our troops were attacking the Germans to the northeast and thought that the enemy would probably be so heavily engaged, they would not waste an artillery shell on only one jeep. Since my duties required me to study the nature of the road and the ground to the north, I rashly passed through the south entrance of the Mousetrap with my jeep and driver. We had proceeded slowly along the road only a few hundred yards when suddenly a single enemy artillery shell roared over our heads and landed approximately one hundred yards directly behind us.

Instantly, I realized that a German artillery battery of four guns was zeroing in on our jeep. (This procedure involved firing a single observed artillery shell from a range of three or four miles, observing where it hit the ground in relation to the desired target, then splitting the estimated distance in half, between the target and the impact of the shell, and firing a second observed shell much closer to the target, then finally splitting the distance in half between the impact of the second shell and the target, after which all four guns in the artillery battery would rapidly fire several shells each on the target until it was destroyed.)

The jeep driver didn't need any instructions from me on what to do. He instantly turned the jeep around and proceeded at top jeep speed directly to the rear. By the time the second zeroing-in enemy shell landed, we had travelled at least two hundred yards to the rear beyond where the first shell had landed, thereby making good our escape from a close brush with quick destruction. Luckily for both of us, the Germans had not fired on our jeep with one of their deadly accurate 88-mm antitank guns.

At this time the 135th Infantry was in reserve protecting the flanks of the 168th Infantry, which was proceeding in a series of skillfully executed night attacks through the olive tree-covered hills on the eastern edge of the Mousetrap. The 135th seized Eddikehila and Chouigui Pass and drove the Germans from the hills, making it possible for our troops to travel, for the first time, on the road in the valley. Meanwhile, the First Battalion had slowly followed the main attacking force to prevent the Germans from counterattacking and destroying them.

On the night of 8 May, the First Battalion was ordered to proceed through Chouigui Pass and seize the town of Chouigui four miles to the east. The attack was postponed until 9 May when we moved through the pass and occupied the shell-torn village of Chouigui without resistance.

On 9 May we received our last attack order of the Tunisian campaign. We were to move several miles north and attack the small groups of fanatical Germans who still resisted in the hills.

Before issuing his attack order to the battalion commanders of the 135th Infantry, Colonel Ward, the regimental commander, directed Lieutenant Colonel Miller and me to report to him at his observation post on a hill from which we could observe clearly, for several miles, the hills and roads to the north of us.

After discussing briefly the overall tactical and strategic situation of the war in North Africa, Colonel Ward informed us that he was reluctant to have his entire regiment (of three thousand men) attack the Germans in the hills (who had been bypassed by the main body of the attacking American army). He stated that before moving forward in another attack, he wanted me to take a jeep and driver, with a large white flag on a staff conspicuously displayed in the jeep, and that my mission was to move forward into the hills and inform the German commander of the futility of further resistance since his troops were completely isolated and about to be attacked by an entire infantry regiment. I was then instructed to try to persuade him to surrender immediately.

Since the war in North Africa was almost over, I was not particularly anxious to test my diplomatic skill on such a mission. Nevertheless, I prepared to leave immediately. However, just as I was ready to depart, Colonel Ward received the joyful news that both Tunis and Bizerte had been captured by our Allied forces and all enemy resistance had crumbled (including that of the enemy groups in the hills to our north) except that in the sector of the British Eighth Army on the Cape Bon peninsula in the extreme northeastern part of Tunisia. Colonel Ward immediately cancelled my mission, and I joyfully returned to my battalion area.

On 13 May 1943 the final victory in North Africa was achieved, after six months of bitterly contested war. The last of the Germans and Italians surrendered to the British Eighth Army on that date. Approximately three hundred thousand German and Italian soldiers surrendered to the Allied forces during the last four days of the war in North Africa.

The price of the Allied victory in North Africa had been extremely high. Approximately 10,820 Allied soldiers had been killed in action, another 39,575 had been wounded, and 21,415 had been captured or reported missing in action, for a grand total of approximately 71,810 casualties since the Allies had landed at Casablanca, Oran, and Algiers on 8 November 1942.

Chapter XX
Siesta Period

Immediately after the end of fighting in Tunisia, there followed a few days of joyous celebration during which we drank much wine, vermouth, and cognac. We even had the rare opportunity to make occasional visits into the cities of Tunis and Bizerte, and also to the beaches near these cities for a few brief swims in the warm sapphire waters of the Mediterranean Sea.

The day after the organized resistance of the enemy on our front ended, Lieutenant Colonel Miller sent Lieutenants Henley, Drury, and me with two jeeps and drivers to an area about five miles to the northwest to reconnoiter the nature of the ground there as a possible location for our battalion to resume its combat training. While passing over a narrow dirt road through a large wheat field, we suddenly espied two well-armed German infantry soldiers sitting on the ground in the middle of the stalks of ripening wheat on the left of the road. Since they were isolated, surrounded, and outnumbered five to two, they immediately surrendered and turned over their rifles, ammunition, and hand grenades to us without firing a shot and promptly got into our jeeps with us in compliance with our instructions. Both of the young German prisoners spoke English fluently. Both were overjoyed that the war in North Africa had ended and that they would soon be sent to the United States as prisoners of war. During the trip to our battalion headquarters they sang, whistled, and laughed continuously. One of them told me that he had lived for several years before the war in Chicago, Illinois, and that he could hardly wait to return to Chicago to see his friends and relatives in that city.

On the next day we moved with our entire First Battalion through Chouigui Pass into the Mousetrap valley to a position south of Eddekehila where the remaining battalions of the Thirty-fourth Infantry Division were concentrated. Our siesta period was soon interrupted by the arrival of approximately a thousand new replacement soldiers who had been assigned to the 135th Infantry to take the places of the thousand casualties that our regiment suffered during the Tunisian campaign. We settled down to a hard training schedule in the hot, dusty weather. Because of the hot weather, we had to take a two-hour siesta in the shade during the hottest part of each afternoon.

The replacements brought the rumor that the Thirty-fourth Division would soon return to the United States to train recruits in infantry combat tactics. The story was told with such convincing detail that some of us eventually began to believe it.

On 18 May Lieutenant Colonel Miller sent me with a small quartering party to the outskirts of Tunis to select an assembly area for the First Battalion. The 135th Infantry had been selected to represent the American army in Tunisia in a gigantic victory parade on 20 May. Most of us immediately began to wonder what kind of an appearance we would make in the filthy, vermin-infested rags we had worn since our arrival in Tunisia.

We were therefore delightfully surprised when suddenly we were issued complete outfits of brand-new clothes, including socks, underwear, tie, shirt, trousers, and shoes. One of the men said to me, "Sir, is it true that when the big parade is over we must turn our new uniforms back to the government and start wearing our rags again?"

Early on the morning of 20 May, we travelled in large trucks to a previously designated area inside the city limits of Tunis, where the parade was scheduled to start.

We arrived at our place in line among the most cosmopolitan

group of fighting men I had ever seen. There were units of the British Coldstream Guards; battalions from the British Eighth Army; Gurkhas from India; Scottish Highlanders in colorful kilts; turbaned Moroccan Goumiers; huge six-foot tall black Senegalese warriors from the French Sudan; smart Spahi Algerian cavalry troops; fighting French troops; and several units of the French Foreign Legion, fresh from the desert.

On the morning of 20 May, we swung with smart precision down the broad palm-lined streets of Tunis to the strains of John Philip Sousa's "Stars and Stripes Forever," breathing deeply of the perfumed air from the roses, which covered the walls, fences, and gardens of Tunis.

Along our route of march through the main street of Tunis, thousands of men, women, and children were crowded. They sat on fences, in trees, and on the tops of buildings. Cries from every throat of *"Vive L'Amérique"* (long live America) rose to a deafening roar as we were pelted from all sides by a constant shower of roses. Unfortunately, we had lived so long in the mud and dirt that it was difficult for us to play the role of triumphant liberators. However, the pomp and the pageantry were inspiring.

The climax of the parade occurred when hundreds of Flying Fortresses swooped down from the sky with a deafening roar just above our heads, dipping their wings in salute as they passed General Eisenhower and General Giraud in the reviewing stand.

Shortly after the parade, we climbed aboard large trucks and started our return journey to our hot, dusty bivouac area in the hinterlands several miles from Tunis. As our trucks jolted roughly along a narrow, hot, dry, dusty dirt road in northern Tunisia, the words of Rudyard Kipling's famous poem "Recessional" kept running through my mind. The first four stanzas of this great poem, written in 1897 when the might and majesty of the British empire were at their zenith, are quoted here, with the hope that they will convey to our readers a sobering message of humility that none will ever forget.

119

Recessional
June 22, 1897

God of our fathers, known of old,
   Lord of our far-flung battle-line,
Beneath whose awful Hand we hold
   Dominion over palm and pine—
Lord God of Hosts, be with us yet,
Lest we forget—lest we forget!

The tumult and the shouting dies,
   The captains and the kings depart:
Still stands Thine ancient sacrifice,
   An humble and a contrite heart.
Lord God of Hosts, be with us yet,
Lest we forget—lest we forget!

Far-call'd our navies melt away,
   On dune and headland sinks the fire:
Lo, all our pomp of yesterday
   Is one with Nineveh and Tyre!
Judge of the Nations, spare us yet,
Lest we forget—lest we forget!

If, drunk with sight of power, we loose
   Wild tongues that have not Thee in awe,
Such boastings as the Gentiles use,
   Or lesser breeds without the Law—
Lord God of Hosts, be with us yet,
Lest we forget—lest we forget!

Chapter XXI
School Days Again—in North Africa

From 21 May to 28 June, I was relieved from the First Battalion and placed on temporary duty as an instructor with the Infantry School of the Thirty-fourth Division, which was operated by Brig. Gen. Benjamin Caffey, our assistant division commander. The school was organized to give all officers and NCOs (noncommissioned officers) in the division specialized training in the infantry combat techniques that our soldiers had learned in the recent fighting.

The weather was so hot we had to discontinue training in the afternoons. This gave us frequent opportunity to go bathing in the Mediterranean Sea.

Because of its close proximity to the village of Chouigui, our school was immediately named "Chouigui U." The high level of training for infantry troops soon bore out the university rating the wiseacres had given to it.

On 28 June 1943, I received the unexpected news that I was promoted to captain in the Army of the United States with date of rank from 6 June 1943. Also, on that date, I was relieved from my instructional duties with Chouigui U and returned to my job as S-3 of the First Battalion. We had instructed only one class of students for five weeks. It was now time to resume intensive preparation to enter battle again.

Shortly after my return to my unit, I was directed to report to the village of Port Aux Poules on the seashore west of Oran where the Fifth U.S. Army had organized an Invasion Training Center to

121

teach amphibious assault techniques. Approximately two hundred officers and enlisted men from the Thirty-fourth Infantry Division were selected to take a seven-day course at the Invasion Training Center. We departed in a long motor convoy early on 29 June.

I rode in a command car with Maj. Roland Anderson, Capt. Donald C. Landon, and Capt. Ray Erikson. We frequently bought cantaloupes and overripe figs from the Arabs along the way, who invariably charged us three times the value of the fruit.

We arrived at our destination on 3 July and were assigned to comfortable cots in well-ventilated tents close to the seashore. We were then given a three-day-pass to Oran, where we soon found that the base section troops occupied all the finest hotels in the city and it was impossible to obtain a place to sleep. I slept the night of 4 July on the floor of an Army truck. On 5 July, I returned in disgust to Port Aux Poules.

Before my visit to Oran, I had not understood any of the reasons for the smoldering hatred that existed between the base section troops on the one hand and the combat troops on the other hand; nor had I been able to understand why, at the slightest provocation, this hatred sometimes flared into fistfights and bar-room brawls, with the combat troops sometimes being forcibly taken into custody of the base section military police.

I knew that the living conditions of combat infantry soldiers in Tunisia had been brutal and dangerous, but during the heavy fighting of the Tunisian campaign, the troops who fought there did not complain about their wretched lot. Because of the difficulty of supplying and reinforcing them over the long communications routes leading from Algiers, they often remained in the front lines for sixty consecutive days with little or no relief, their clothing badly torn, and their only sustenance, three meals of C rations (hash for breakfast, beans for dinner, stew for supper) per day. However, they were inured to living a hard, tough life. They accepted their lot cheerfully because they had not yet suffered from the bitterness that was engendered later when they were afforded the opportunity of making a comparison between the living conditions they had so long endured with those of the personnel of the base sections.

After the fighting in Tunisia ended, the combat troops sometimes had a chance to make brief visits to several of the large cities of North Africa. On these occasions they suddenly discovered that, while they had suffered excruciatingly from cold, a poor diet, and a shortage of cigarettes, the base section troops had been living comfortably in fine hotels, subsisting on adequate rations augmented with canned peaches and fruit cocktail, with the opportunity to purchase every day all the leading brands of cigarettes they could smoke. This sudden discovery by combat veterans, who had lived for weeks in cold mud and whose every waking moment had for so long been a constant struggle to avoid sudden, violent death, resulted in their feeling bitter toward the base section troops. In this state of mind, it was perhaps inevitable that the combat troops would be much quicker to engage in fistfights with the base section troops than to give them full recognition and credit for the magnificent job they were doing by working long, gruelling hours to keep the combat soldiers well supplied with the necessary guns, ammunition, and equipment to end the war as soon as possible.

In a few cases, the bitterness that existed between base section and combat troops undermined the morale of the fighting men. In these cases the combat infantrymen began to feel self-pity and to wonder if they were not stupid suckers and fools for going back to face enemy bullets in the mud and dirt of the front lines. Later, when they forced themselves to return to the front, a few of them suffered such low morale they either became malingerers or actual psychoneurotics, all too ready to call it quits even at the risk of suffering court-martial and disgrace.

The bad feeling between the combat and base section soldiers often had a harmful effect upon infantry replacements before they had the chance to hear a single shot fired in anger. Before they arrived at the front, they sometimes heard tall tales of blood and thunder, and were thoroughly indoctrinated with the poisonous

123

propaganda of the martyrlike life of the combat infantryman with all the world against him while the base section troops lived in unbelievable luxury far to the rear beyond the range of enemy bombers in beautiful villas with plenty of wine, pretty women, and champagne. When subjected to such propaganda, it was difficult for a newly arrived infantry replacement to maintain a normal, confident outlook toward his impending entry into battle against a ruthless enemy.

In retrospect, I am convinced that combat troops should not be mollycoddled nor should their hard luck at being combat fighting men be unduly publicized. Combat cartoons and publications should not engender self-pity and persecution complexes in combat soldiers. On the contrary, every available means should be used to make the combat soldier feel hard, tough, and superior to every other type of soldier and that his is a rare privilege to fight in the forefront of battle for his country.

On 6 July, after a three-day period of inactivity, we attended our first classes at the Invasion Training Center. Our instruction was ably presented by a well-qualified staff of U.S. Army officers. We received a thorough indoctrination in the techniques of amphibious warfare and, for the first time, had the chance to see large amphibious trucks with a capability of travelling equally well on land or on water.

The instruction at Port Aux Poules ended on 10 July. On the following day, we started our return journey to Tunisia to rejoin our battalion. The weather was fair throughout our trip, which was most pleasant and enjoyable.

Our return journey to Tunisia was uneventful except for one enchanted evening a few of us spent in a rather unusual restaurant at the small seaport town of Tenes, a few miles west of Algiers. Late in the afternoon of our first day of travel, a group of about fifteen or twenty officers assembled in a small restaurant in Tenes, on a high hill overlooking the Mediterranean Sea. The interior of the restaurant was brilliantly lighted and tastefully decorated. Aside from the American soldiers there were only a few Frenchmen and their lady friends present. Among these, I noticed sitting in a corner of the restaurant, a handsome young French corporal and his beautiful fiancée. Almost immediately, the French soldier and his lady began to sing romantic songs to each other. Soon the proprietor of the restaurant entered the room and also sang a delightful song while all present listened in rapt attention; then each of the three pretty waitresses in her turn, also sang songs. Following the thunderous applause, the Americans, not wanting to be outdone, immediately launched into lusty renditions of "I've Been Working on the Railroad" and "Down by the Old Mill Stream," accompanied by an accordion that Major Anderson's jeep driver carried with him. He produced it at the right psychological moment to prevent the American officers from losing face because of a lack of musical talent.

We rejoined the 135th Infantry in Tunisia on 14 July without further incident.

Chapter XXII
Company Commander

Immediately upon my arrival in Tunisia, I was informed of my new assignment as commanding officer of Company C, 135th Infantry, to replace Capt. Charles Fanning, who had returned to the United States on the newly inaugurated policy of rotating combat experienced officers to train recruits.

I had not yet commanded a rifle company, but my job was much easier because of the splendid officers and noncommissioned officers in my new company. The officers were 1st Lt. Gail Bell and Second Lieutenants Atkinson, Sale, Lindstrand, and Maness. Some of the outstanding noncommissioned officers were 1st Sgt. Gustave N. Suck and Staff Sergeants Ivan L. Glover, Windsor, and Julian L. Greenwood.

My company was in an olive grove near the seacoast at this time. Little training was in progress since the Thirty-fourth Division had just been alerted to go by rail to the Invasion Training Center near Oran to pursue amphibious training. I thus had a good opportunity to get acquainted gradually with my subordinates in C Company.

On 20 July we boarded trucks and were hauled to the city of Tunis where we clambered aboard a dirty, ill-smelling freight train. We were so tightly crowded it was impossible for anyone to stretch himself out at full length. Our bed was the hard floor of the freight cars. Our food consisted only of C rations.

Because our train moved slowly, we did not arrive in Oran until dark on 25 July. Meanwhile, we relieved the monotony of our

C-ration diet and augmented our rations by bartering with the Arabs along the route for figs, oranges, tomatoes, cantaloupes, and watermelons.

Because of the reaction of our men to the severe conditions of recently ended combat, it was difficult to enforce discipline on the long train; therefore, it was almost impossible to prevent some of the personnel from hurling tomatoes and melon rinds at the Arabs and from frequently yelling loudly, "Vive de Gaulle" and "Vive Giraud," as we passed through the many small villages along our route of travel. (At this time Gen. Charles de Gaulle and Gen. Henri Giraud were the joint political leaders of North Africa, which was then governed by French authorities.)

A few miles east of Oran our train stopped near the large base of La Senia Airport. All eyes immediately rested on several stacks of canned peaches, pears, and fruit cocktail next to a quartermaster depot near the train.

The temptation to seize some of this delicious food was too much for our hardened combat veterans who had subsisted almost solely on C rations for five months. Some of the enlisted men and officers surged from the train and overwhelmed the guards posted round the food supplies and seized large quantities of canned fruit.

Before the train could resume its journey, an irate quartermaster officer climbed aboard and, fuming with rage, demanded to see the train commander. Unfortunately neither the train commander nor the culprits could be located and the quartermaster officer was left standing empty-handed beside the train as it started with a violent lurch.

After the train pulled out of the station, a smiling Frenchwoman stood in her yard on the outskirts of the town and laughingly tried to dodge a deluge of cans of C rations which were tossed to her in an unending stream from the entire length of the train. In the space of a few seconds, she received enough food to last her an entire year.

We arrived in Oran late at night and loaded on trucks. After a long ride through the darkness, we arrived at our bivouac area on the top of a dusty hill near the village of Ain-El-Turk by the sea.

The next afternoon, the inspector general of the Thirty-fourth Division called on us formally and informed us that each officer had to swear that he had not taken or eaten any of the fruit stolen at La Senia Airport or else we would have to pay for the fruit. Rather than swear a statement of dubious veracity, each officer voluntarily contributed five dollars to pay for the fruit, which amounted to a total of $180.

We remained in our barren location for about two weeks and pursued specialized assault training in the morning, made long hikes in the afternoons, and at night conducted attack problems.

On 12 August we moved thirty-five miles inland to a wooded area near Sidi-bel-Abbès where we engaged in field exercises that included several night problems. We also continued our hikes and individual hardening training. We had movies each night.

On 28 August, after finishing our training at Sidi-bel-Abbès, we moved to a large vineyard by the Mediterranean Sea near Ain El Turk, where we boarded a ship and received several days of amphibious landing exercises. Next, we moved back to our bivouac area in the vineyard where we received the news that Italy had finally been knocked out of the war.

When first received, this was glorious news. However, within a few days, Adolf Hitler sent several of his finest infantry and armored divisions into Italy and occupied the entire country. When these divisions were reinforced and placed into defensive positions in the mountains of Italy under the superb leadership of one of Hitler's finest combat commanders, Field Marshal Albert Kesselring, we realized that we would soon be sent across the Mediterranean Sea to reinforce the gallant Thirty-sixth Infantry Division, which was, in early September 1943, engaged in a desperate battle with the Germans at Salerno beachhead in Italy.

Chapter XXIII
Sunny Italy

On 15 September, we moved to Oran and boarded a ship for Italy.

After an uneventful voyage of five days, we touched the Italian shore at the village of Paestum near the mouth of the Sele River on Salerno Beach. Here, the Thirty-sixth Division had struggled bitterly against the Germans only a few days before. We were originally scheduled to land at Naples, but because it was still in enemy hands we had to land directly on the beach at Salerno. Since the battle had moved a few miles to the north, we did not engage in any fighting.

Most of our transportation had not arrived from Africa, so we made a long march on a dusty road before we reached our bivouac area in a large open field. At first Italy reminded me of Tunisia. There was plenty of dust on the roads, few trees, and the weather was so hot, heat waves rose from the barren hills that surrounded Salerno. In the distance, several huge mountains towered toward the sky.

We remained several days in the bivouac area under continuous alert to move to the front. The weather was extremely hot. At night, swarms of mosquitos hovered over us. The hot weather suddenly changed during the last three days of September, when a violent storm accompanied by high winds and heavy rainfall caused the air to cool and the dust to turn into a sea of sticky mud.

On 30 September, we were finally told that we would move to the front by truck early the next morning.

From 1 to 8 October we were in division reserve. We moved forward slowly behind the troops of the assaulting regiments and gradually away from the seashore over a narrow, rocky road which wound through the steep mountains of southern Italy.

Because the Germans had destroyed the bridges along our route, our progress was slow. However, we had an excellent opportunity to observe Italy. Most of the valleys were divided into small farms, which were often covered with vineyards. The houses, like those in North Africa and Ireland, were of stone. The mountains and hills were steep and rocky, but unlike those in Africa, they were covered with chestnut, olive, and oak trees. Often we saw, perched high on a steep mountain, an Italian village rising in white contrast to the blue skies. Upon closer approach, the village usually proved to be a dirty conglomeration of stone huts with steep, narrow streets.

The majority of the people were delighted to see us. Many of them rushed out, threw their arms around our necks, and yelled, *"Paisan!"* Some gave us bread, grapes, wine, figs, and English walnuts. In return, we shared our C rations with them, which they promptly declared to be the best food they had ever eaten.

Many American soldiers spoke Italian fluently, which made the language barrier no problem at all. Often we halted to rest in one of the villages. When I sat on the ground, like the rest of the men, the Italians frequently ran up to me with a chair and yelled, *"Officiel, Officiel!"* It was hard for them to get used to seeing an Army officer so undignified as to sit on the ground. In European armies such a thing was unheard of.

Although their houses were small, with but little land available for farming, the average Italian family had at least ten children who were poorly dressed and seemed to be on the verge of starvation. The masses of the people were so impoverished, it seemed that only a few people had most of the wealth.

Chapter XXIV
The First Crossing of the Volturno

If you should ask an elementary school student what is the longest river in the world, he would probably tell you that it is the Missouri-Mississippi. On the other hand, if you ask a World War II veteran of the 135th Infantry who fought in Italy the same question, he will answer without hesitation, "The Volturno is the longest river in the world." He believes this because, in a period of only twenty-four days, the 135th Infantry made three crossings of the Volturno River. Each crossing was made in darkness through deep, cold water, wading in the face of enemy artillery, rifle, and machine-gun fire. To anyone who participated in those three crossings, the Volturno will always be the longest river in the world.

On the night of 8 October, we started on foot toward the Volturno River some ten miles ahead of us. We were to relieve a battalion of the Third Infantry Division, which had been fighting for almost a month. On 9 October we occupied a defensive position on the south bank of the river. Our position was near the crests of several wooded hills that rose steeply from the water's edge. On the other side of the river, on a steep wooded hill, were the Germans. Their hill was much steeper and higher than the one on which we were located. This afforded them excellent observation of our positions. The Germans were quick to react. From time to time they covered our positions with artillery fire that had little effect. The trees offered us excellent concealment and our foxholes protected us from the shell fragments.

We spent the time from 9 to 12 October preparing to cross the

Volturno River and attack the Germans. Several patrols were sent out each night to select routes of approach to the river, to test its depth, and to see if anything could be determined concerning the German defensive positions on the other side of the river.

At 0200 hours on 13 October, the First Battalion, 135th Infantry, started moving toward the banks of the Volturno. Company B was to cross on the left and move rapidly into the hills, while Company A was to cross five hundred yards upstream and converge on a wooded ridge on the far side of the river. The ridge seemed to be heavily defended by the Germans.

Since I had been promoted only recently from first lieutenant to captain and designated as commanding officer of Company C, I had not yet led an infantry rifle company in combat. For this reason, I was anxious to learn what our first combat mission would be.

Company C was given the mission of following closely behind Company A, prepared either to attack to the right of Company A, or to move in between Company A and Company B and seize the part of the objective between the two companies. The assault on the hill and the crossing of the river were to be preceded by a heavy mortar and artillery barrage.

As we moved slowly down the hill to the river, we walked in single file between the steep, narrow banks of a small dirt road. The moon shone so brightly that we assumed an interval between men of from three to five yards. We proceeded past a shattered house, crossed a railroad that paralleled the river, and prepared to rush across a hard-surfaced highway near the river. Several shells whistled over our heads and landed about 150 yards to our rear. I ordered my men to take cover in the ditch along the road and then to start crossing the road, rushing in groups of two and three. Evidently the Germans could not see us, as the move was completed without casualties. We halted briefly in a large vineyard about two hundred yards from the road and waited while our own artillery laid down a heavy barrage on the hills across the river.

When the shelling ceased, we moved rapidly through the

darkness to the edge of the water and started to cross by holding on to a large rope strung over it by Company A, which had already crossed the river. The water was only armpit deep, but it was both swift and cold. As I grasped the rope firmly with both hands, I heard a loud explosion about fifty to seventy-five yards ahead of me on the German side of the river. Since the moon had now gone down, it was so dark I could not see the explosion; however, the water splashed all about me as several pieces of shrapnel whined past my ears. I hurried across the river and found out that one of the men in Company A had detonated an enemy antipersonnel mine attached to a large Teller antitank mine.

For a few minutes, I took the lead in my company, then fell back behind the first platoon, urging the men all along the line to walk closely in the footsteps of the men of A Company, who were now moving slowly ahead of us through a wooded gully that led onto the hill in front of us. Our route onto the hill was strewn with dead and wounded men of Company A who had fallen in the extensive field of antipersonnel mines the Germans had placed with diabolical cleverness along the path through the gully. We made such slow progress that it was soon almost daylight.

Meanwhile, the battalion commander contacted me.

"Captain Bailey," he ordered, "move your company out of this, d——n gulley at once, cross that open plowed field up ahead, and get into the hills and on the objective as soon as possible. Get your company deployed in a line of skirmishers and out of this d——n column formation."

I moved forward as rapidly as I could and contacted the leader of the leading squad of the company and started with him across the open plowed field that lay between us and the wooded hill to our front. We crossed almost the entire field successfully without a shot being fired at us and were approaching a road that bordered the woods when an enemy machine gun opened fire on us from the woods about fifty yards ahead.

We immediately hit the dirt and lay flat on our stomachs in the middle of the open field. It was now almost daylight and getting lighter with each passing second. In my haste, I had run off and left my radio operator with his S.C.R. 536 radio far behind me. I, therefore, had no means of contacting my platoon leaders or of exercising any control over my company. Out of the company of 185 men, I controlled only one squad of twelve men. With much fear and some misgiving, I ordered the squad leader to have his men fix bayonets. When this was done, at my signal, we rose to our feet and dashed with loud yells across the road and into the woods. Instead of firing at us as we expected them to do, the German machine-gun crew of only two men came out with their hands up and surrendered without firing another shot.

We moved farther into the hills to consolidate our objective as quickly as possible.

While crossing the road, I had noticed a dead German soldier lying beside his motorcycle. He was dirty and muddy and so full of bullet holes he looked as if he had been dead for several days. Later, First Lieutenant Lyons, commanding officer of Company A, told me that at the approach of his men, the German had jumped astride his motorcycle, started the motor, then paused long enough to empty his machine pistol at the advancing Americans. At this action, about twenty-five riflemen emptied their weapons into the German, thus preventing his warning the main body of Germans of our attack.

Upon my arrival on the hill, I began immediately to rally my men. In a few minutes, Lieutenants Stokes and Johnson joined me and told me that their platoons were disposed in the woods to the right and that they had suffered no casualties, but had captured five Germans.

I ordered the three rifle platoon leaders to have their men dig foxholes, to make contact with Companies A and B, and to prepare for a counterattack.

I was unable to locate my weapons platoon commanded by Lieutenant Atkins or the headquarters and command group commanded by Lieutenant Bell, the company executive officer. Later, I learned that these two groups, bringing up the rear, had been almost destroyed by an enemy mine detonated at the edge of the river. Nine men were killed and fourteen severely wounded. Among the dead was 1st Sgt. Gustave N. Suck, whose posthumous battlefield promotion to the grade of second lieutenant for conspicuous bravery in action arrived the day after his death. His loss created a gap in the ranks of Company C that was impossible to fill, although an able man, Sergeant Young, immediately became first sergeant.

After a hasty reorganization, word reached us that Company A had suffered extremely heavy casualties by enemy mine action. Company B slipped through a gap between a small group of some twenty-seven Germans, which lay in ambush for them, and the minefield through which Companies A and C had paid so heavy a toll in their crossing. The sole action of Company B was a small one caused by three or four insolent German soldiers who loudly challenged the American "pigs" of Company B to come in and get them. The Americans readily accommodated the Germans by storming in and killing all of them. In this attack about fifty Germans, with the aid of a large field of cleverly placed antipersonnel mines, were able to inflict heavy casualties on 890 attacking Americans. Evidently their mission had only been to delay our advance briefly, then withdraw several miles ahead of us to higher ground where they could observe us as we approached and again inflict heavy casualties on us before withdrawing again.

Throughout the day we remained near the crest of the wooded hill overlooking the Volturno River. At noon the Germans launched a small counterattack against Company B. It was easily repulsed. During the afternoon they covered the hill with artillery fire that caused only a few casualties. Later, an Italian informed us that the deep wooded ravines on the route of advance ahead of us were heavily mined by the Germans and that we ought to circle wide to the left and bypass the ravines.

We had crossed the river near the village of Amorisi where the

135

river made a sharp bend west toward the Mediterranean Sea. We thus crossed the river from south to north and headed in a direction across country roughly parallel to the river on its west bank.

On the night of 13 October, we made a wide swing to the left of the minefields and trudged forward for most of the rest of the night, halting just before dawn on the crest of a low wooded ridge without meeting any Germans. During most of the next day, we moved slowly forward across wooded hills still following the winding course of the Volturno River. During the day, two German planes flew low over us and strafed our column with machine-gun fire, but failed to hit anyone.

For several days we moved rapidly forward during day and night through low hills covered with vineyards and sparse woods until we arrived in the midst of a large vineyard on a gently sloping hill near the town of Dragoni, on the banks of the Volturno River. We remained all day and rested, meanwhile receiving word that we would again cross the Volturno River and continue moving north on its east bank.

Chapter XXV
The Second Crossing of the Volturno

Shortly after dark, on 18 October, we again plunged into the cold waters of the Volturno River and started for the far bank. This time the water was so deep it reached to my armpits. However, we were fortunate in meeting no enemy resistance. We went into an assembly area after marching about a thousand yards on the flat ground on the east bank of the river.

The sky was heavily overcast and the night was so dark, that, as I stumbled along, I suddenly fell into a deep pond full of muddy water. Fortunately, however, I was able to enter a nearby farmhouse and dry by a roaring fire in the kitchen. The Italian also gave me some bread, figs, and delicious wine. Meanwhile, the battalion commanding officer called his company commanders into the kitchen of the farmhouse and, pointing to a map, told us we would move out at 0200 hours the next morning along the left side of the road, which led across the flat valley and through the village of Alife, and seize a position in the wooded hills on the other side of the valley. I had the mission of leading the battalion with Company C.

After a few hours of troubled sleep, we moved off promptly at 0200 with a platoon of tanks accompanying us. It was so dark our progress was slow. When dawn broke, we were still in the open, in the middle of the broad valley. However, a thick fog concealed us from the view of the Germans in the hills. Some tall aspen trees, deep ravines, and vineyards gave us both concealment and cover.

The battalion commander meanwhile gave Company A the

mission of moving ahead of Company C, crossing the road that paralleled the valley, and moving as rapidly as possible into the hills. As Company A tried to cross the road, several machine guns opened fire on it from the woods on the far side of the road. At about this time, an excited Italian civilian rushed up and, with frantic gesticulations and flailing of arms, told Lieutenant Colonel Miller that a large force of Germans with many machine guns was surrounding us. Meanwhile, the fog suddenly lifted and Lieutenant Colonel Miller ordered everybody to halt and dig foxholes until we could find out how much artillery the Germans had in the hills. We soon found out. They laid a heavy concentration of shells on us, which caused several casualties including Major Shinn and First Lieutenant Openshaw, both of whom were evacuated to the hospital. Meanwhile Colonel Ward, the regimental commander, visited us and ordered us to remain temporarily in our present positions. During this time seventeen enemy tanks started to attack us from up the valley, but all the artillery in the Thirty-fourth Division, and some additional artillery from the corps, stopped the attack and knocked out several of the tanks. The ensuing afternoon was relatively quiet.

The next day the enemy laid down heavy artillery fire on us until afternoon when the battalion commander ordered me to take my company at once into the hills. If I should make it okay, the remainder of the battalion was to follow. I moved out with my company behind me in single file, wading through the middle of a small creek with steep, vertical banks offering excellent cover. We proceeded rapidly for several hundred yards, went under a bridge, and were finally stopped by a heavy barrage of enemy shells. I halted, sent a message to the battalion commander, to ask him to postpone the move until after dark. He agreed. After dark I led the battalion into the hills without any casualties, and we resumed a defensive position.

We continued to move forward for several days meeting little resistance, meanwhile staying in the olive tree-covered hills. During this time we passed through the village of St. Angelo and Raviscaninia and approached the town of Pratella on the main highway among several wooded hills.

On the afternoon of 26 October, the First Battalion was near the crest of a high mountain east of the Volturno River. Between our positions and Pratella a long wooded ridge in the shape of a sugarloaf occupied a diagonal position in front of us. To our left the ridge was heavily wooded and rose in a steep hill to a height of over a thousand meters. As I faced the hill, a saddle lay between it and a lower, barren, rocky hill leading to the right. Coming out from Pratella and swinging to the right of both hills, a narrow paved road led into the hills and then swung back between our positions and the two-hilled ridge.

The battalion commanding officer informed me that we would seize Pratella shortly after daylight the next morning, with Company C moving through the saddle between the two hills and Company B swinging around to the left of the high wooded hill, with Company A in reserve.

At 0200 hours, I woke my company and started through the darkness toward the objective. I paused briefly at the Third Battalion Command Post and was informed that a roadblock had been placed along the road ahead of me to prevent tanks or armored cars from hitting my company as we crossed the road.

I continued down the mountain, making extremely slow progress until dawn. Although it was broad daylight, a heavy fog hugged the ground. As I approached the road, I sent out a patrol to investigate. When the all-clear report was given, I crossed the road just behind my lead squad and we proceeded rapidly through the woods along a narrow path to the saddle where we were able to obtain an excellent view of the town we were to attack, less than a thousand yards ahead of us. I immediately sent for my platoon leaders to issue them the order to attack the town.

Suddenly, I heard firing about a thousand yards behind me. My entire company was strung out in single file along the path behind me. In a few minutes my two leading platoon leaders arrived and advised me that my third and fourth platoons were cut off from the rest of the company by five German tanks and were unable to cross the road. While I was trying to decide what to do, an excited Italian arrived and told me a large force of Germans with machine guns was coming round the rocky hill to my right rear to cut me off and that another large force of Germans was entrenched on top of the thousand-foot wooded hill to my left. Meanwhile, an aged Italian man rushed out, threw his arms round my neck, and kissed me on both cheeks. I immediately issued orders for my two platoons to dig foxholes, forming a perimeter defense around the crest of the rocky hill. We waited for several minutes until we saw a large German patrol approaching us from the town of Pratella. I ordered my men not to fire on the patrol until it was almost upon us. Someone fired prematurely on the patrol at long range and the Germans escaped into the town.

At this turn of affairs, I figured that the patrol would inform the Germans in the town of our location, so we immediately moved out of our positions toward the crest of the high, wooded hill. I meanwhile advised the battalion commander by radio and by written message of my location and of my actions and received his permission to call off the attack on the town since Company B had been held up and was unable to cross the road.

We had almost reached the top of the hill when we were stopped by heavy small arms fire, whereupon we moved halfway down the hill and went again into defensive positions concealed in the woods. We remained in observation of the enemy in Pratella, who were now loading up on large, heavy trucks and proceeding to move out of the town. I repeatedly requested artillery fire to be laid on the Germans, but my radio finally went dead and no fire was brought down on the Germans. Meanwhile, our food supply gave out and we had no water. At dark, I started to withdraw down the path to the rear. When I had proceeded about a hundred yards, I met

First Lieutenant Lyons from Company A with a message from the battalion commander ordering me to withdraw.

We continued to the rear of the wooded hill and went into battalion reserve in pitch darkness. In the middle of the night an enemy shell hit in the area and killed one of my men lying on top of the ground. I had ordered everyone to dig foxholes, but it was too dark for me to see if all complied with my order.

During the last few days of October and the first days of November, we moved forward through large vineyards, meeting with little resistance until we again approached the Volturno River.

Chapter XXVI
The Third Crossing of the Volturno

At dusk on the afternoon of 5 November, we started wading through the cold waters of the Volturno River for the third time in twenty-four days. We met no enemy fire, but on reaching the west bank, we entered extensive minefields. The 168th Infantry had already passed through the area after suffering heavy casualties and had laid behind them long lines of white engineer tape to guide us.

We moved forward carefully and went into an assembly area in an olive grove on a steep mountain covered with rocks. We had no blankets, which caused us intense discomfort because of the chilling wind that blew steadily all night. Things warmed up, however, when the Germans laid a heavy mortar barrage among us, killing one sergeant and wounding several other soldiers.

On the following morning, we rose long before daylight. My company was in battalion reserve so we moved at a snail's pace at the rear of the battalion all day without being committed to action. We were among steep, conical, olive tree-covered hills. I received word at about 1600 hours to move forward for the order to attack a hill called 609. Before I reached the top of the hill, I received an order to report back to the C Company kitchen and prepare to go to Sorrento, an Italian summer resort, for four days' rest. I never more willingly complied with an order.

I spent four delightful days at Sorrento. However, I spent most of my time resting. I slept on a soft feather bed between clean sheets. I hadn't seen a bed in more than a year, so when sightseeing tours were arranged to visit Mount Vesuvius and the Isle of Capri, I was not even slightly interested.

When I returned to Company C, which was commanded during my absence by 1st Lt. Gail Bell, I found that the First Battalion had moved forward several hundred yards, had captured many prisoners, and was now in some tall, wooded mountains with snow on their summits.

Chapter XXVII
Mountains, Rain, and Mud

The mountains, near the village of Montequilla where we were now located, were extremely rugged. The roads were little more than narrow, winding, dirt trails. It was necessary to organize mule trains in order to carry supplies to our troops over these trails.

Prior to 14 November, the weather in Italy had been beautiful and sunny. The brilliant red and gold in the autumn leaves had added some cheer to our lives. Moreover, most of our fighting had not been too severe.

On 14 November a steady downpour of rain commenced and fell every day for a month. The roads became deeply rutted quagmires of the stickiest, slimiest mud I have ever tried to wade through. At this time the Germans were occupying heavily fortified positions in the rugged mountains in front of us. They called this their "winter line." Thus, the combination of miserable weather, rugged mountains, and a determined, skillful enemy slowed our advance to a standstill.

From 14 through 17 of November the First Battalion was in regimental reserve, occupying several wooded hills and small ridges situated several hundred yards behind the main line of resistance of the 135th Infantry Regiment. This was a relatively quiet period in which we received no incoming mortar or artillery fire and during which we were not even required to send out any patrols to probe the enemy positions, which were located on a steep rocky mountain called Pantano. Thus, my exhausted men were provided a brief period of approximately four days of surcease from enemy shelling, which had been almost continuous for all of us since the night of October 13 when we waded for the first time through the cold, turgid waters of the Volturno River.

Since no war can be won by sitting and occupying defensive positions indefinitely, I received orders on 18 November to move forward with my company along a narrow, winding road that led over the crest of a steep rocky ridge on the approaches to Mount Pantano. Since the weather was dark and rainy with relatively poor visibility, we were shielded from enemy view and able to move during daylight without being subjected to any enemy fire. We moved into and occupied defensive frontline positions on the wooded forward slopes of the ridge facing Mount Pantano during the afternoon.

We remained in these advanced positions from 18 through 23 November, during which time we were constantly on the alert for either heavy attacks or strong infiltrating enemy combat patrols. Our own patrolling was active, as was that of the enemy. We received some sporadic mortar and artillery fire, but the overcast skies, the rainy mist that fell incessantly, and the dark nights shielded us most of the time from direct enemy observation.

On one or two rare occasions the weather cleared sufficiently for me to see snow on the steep, forest-clad mountains in front of our positions. My company command post was located in an old circular stone building with neither a roof nor a floor. There were, however, several wooden beams extending across the top of the circular wall of the building that were matted with grape vines and provided some small shelter from the cold rain, which fell steadily throughout the days and the nights. Somehow, we managed to start a fire inside our stone walls and keep it going despite the steady rain, thus providing some relief from the frigid winds that incessantly blew from the direction of the snow on Mount Pantano.

Late one afternoon, I received a call on my field telephone from Lieutenant Colonel Miller, commanding officer, First Battalion. He had called to bid me good-bye and tell me that he was

145

returning to the United States on rotation and was being succeeded as battalion commander by Maj. Ray Erickson and Capt. Arnold N. Brandt, commanding officer of Company D, was assuming the job of battalion executive officer.

Late on another afternoon just before darkness, I concluded my remarks to my assembled platoon leaders with instructions to be especially watchful throughout the night for infiltrating German patrols. As was customary, I then gave my platoon leaders the password for the night with the warning, "Tell your sentries to challenge anybody they hear moving in front of our lines by yelling 'Australian' and to fire on anybody who doesn't immediately yell back 'Kangaroo.' "

Later, during the darkest part of that same night, one of the frontline sentries of Company C was aroused to instant alertness by the sudden sharp rustle of leaves and breaking twigs as something sinister moved steadily toward him through the thick underbrush on the steep slopes below his position. Instantly the sentry dropped to the prone position, snapped off the safety of his M-1 rifle and yelled, "Australian!"

Quick as lightning, an unmistakably British-accented voice yelled in reply from the underbrush, "Yes, sir, one Austr-eye-lian and two New Zealanders."

Too surprised to fire as he had been ordered, the astonished sentry directed the intruders to advance and be recognized. A few seconds later, three weary, bedraggled Allied soldiers in tattered uniforms emerged from the underbrush in no-man's land and scrambled up the steep slopes of a rocky ridge into the safety of the American lines occupied by the men of Company C, 135th Infantry Regiment.

One was an Australian! The other two were New Zealanders!

They had been wandering for several days behind the German lines, but somehow had finally made good their escape, carrying with them some valuable information concerning the heavy fortifications being constructed by the Germans in their winter line positions.

We remained in our forward positions on the approaches to Mount Pantano until 24 November. On that day, we received the welcome news to move back to the rear to positions in the Thirty-fourth Division Reserve in the vicinity of the small village of Montequilla, located in a valley at the base of the mountains leading into the Mount Pantano positions. We were all particularly happy at this timing of our move to the rear, because it enabled us to be out of the front lines on Thanksgiving Day and thus afforded us the unexpected opportunity to eat a delicious meal of turkey with the traditional trimmings. During our rather lengthy periods of combat, we had eaten such large quantities of cold C rations that we had viewed the approach of Thanksgiving with an almost fatalistic attitude and had not expected to eat a meal of delicious turkey. Hence, when the unexpected news arrived ordering us to the rear into reserve positions out of range of enemy artillery and mortar fire, we felt that we had plenty to be thankful for on Thanksgiving Day in the mountains of Italy in November 1943.

We remained in division reserve in Montequilla until 27 November. Throughout this period, the weather was cold and rainy. So much rain fell in such a steady stream that we were unable to do any training. It was almost impossible to venture very far outside of our pup tents. All of our clothing was damp and clammy, and the mud was so deep it was extremely difficult to keep either dry or clean, or free of mildew and mold.

Finally on 27 November, we received information that the 135th Infantry Regiment would remain in division reserve for a few more days, but that the First Battalion must furnish one of its companies to move forward to a position a short distance behind the regimental frontline positions. This company was to be designated the patrol company of the regiment and was to have the mission of sending out patrols every day beyond our front lines toward Mount Pantano to obtain as much information as possible as quickly as possible about the German defensive positions on the mountains north of us.

On 27 November, the rifle company commanders of the First Battalion, 135th Infantry, were directed to draw straws to determine who would have the honor of moving forward as the patrol company for the regiment. I drew the unlucky short straw, moved toward Mount Pantano along a narrow, muddy road, and selected for my command post a small stone house about a thousand yards behind the frontline companies of the Third Battalion.

During our stay in this position, it rained in profusion every day. Except for the Company C patrols that went out every day, we had no contact with the enemy.

The house where my command post was located was well concealed from enemy observation. It was built on the right of the road as we faced the front over a steep bank, so that a concrete patio led from the road into the living room. On both sides of the house, the patio fell away in a vertical wall, to a distance of ten feet, among many large, rough rocks strewn on the ground. On days when it did not rain, I ate supper on the patio with the company executive officer, the first sergeant, and several others.

One afternoon I remarked to First Sergeant Young, "Well, Sergeant, I wonder if a man would jump down that ten-foot wall, if an artillery shell should suddenly land near us."

Just as I spoke we heard the loud whistle of several incoming artillery shells. In a split second, I found myself landing on my head and shoulders among the rocks at the base of the vertical wall of the porch. I had reacted so fast that my coffee, powdered eggs, and canned meat were scattered all over the porch floor. Looking round me, I noticed that I had plenty of company. The shells hit near us but did no damage.

During this period Company C suffered the great loss of Staff Sgt. Ivan L. Glover, one of the bravest soldiers I have ever known. He had volunteered for service with the Canadian army in 1939 and had been overseas more than three years. He was lost on the steep slopes of Mount Pantano leading a patrol against the enemy.

Company C rejoined the First Battalion on 30 November. We remained at Montequilla until 4 December and then moved up the steep slopes of Mount Pantano to relieve a battalion of the 168th Infantry, which had just fought one of the bitterest and bloodiest battles in the war.

During the afternoon, in a steady downpour of rain, I struggled wearily up the slick slopes of Mount Pantano with a guide and reconnaissance party of one noncommissioned officer (NCO) from each of my platoons, leaving my company to be brought forward during darkness by Lieutenant Bell. The mountain rose almost straight up for over three thousand feet above the valley floor. Our route was a narrow, winding trail.

The Germans laid an almost continuous barrage of mortar shells along the entire length of the trail. Thus began one of the most gruesome experiences of my life. All along the trail lay the bodies of dead American soldiers, some with jagged holes in their heads, some with torn backs, and some with no visible wounds. As we neared the top of the mountain, the trail became narrower and finally gave out, but the dead bodies became thicker until near the top there must have been at least two hundred haphazardly scattered over the hill. At the top, extending down the other side, lay the bodies of several hundred dead German soldiers who had made a gallant but futile attempt to wrest Mount Pantano from the Americans. Because of the heavy enemy mortar and artillery fire, which fell steadily among us, it was impossible either to move or to bury the dead. The weather was so cold that the bodies lay where they fell and did not decompose.

As soon as possible, I made a reconnaissance of the entire area where my company was to go into its defensive positions. After having made a tentative plan for the tactical disposition of each of the platoons in Company C, I selected the location for my company command post in the same spot as that of the rifle company that was being relieved. I had just remarked to one of my sergeants, who had accompanied me, that I planned to move my gear into the same foxhole that had been occupied by my predecessor, the company commander from the 168th Infantry.

Suddenly, one of the men of the 168th Infantry turned to me and said "Sir, if I were you, I would select another location for my foxhole. My company commander was killed by a mortar shell in this same foxhole you are talking about taking over and moving into."

Although I wasn't sure that lightning would strike twice in the same place, I accepted the sound advice of this combat veteran and selected a new site for my command post and my foxhole, a few yards farther down the hill and echeloned to the right as I faced the frontline positions. The ground was hard and rocky, but I started digging my foxhole between two large rocks, which already protruded perpendicularly part of the way out of the steep slope of the hillside. The two rocks were flat on their sides and separated by a distance of approximately three feet, so I planned to dig as deeply as I could between the two rocks so I could put my shelter half over the top of them initially to keep dry, then later put logs, limbs, and dirt across the tops of the rocks for protection against mortar and artillery fire.

During the remainder of the afternoon, pending the arrival of my company, I had little that I could do but dig. This I did steadily. Steadily throughout the afternoon incoming enemy mortar shells whispered and whistled over my head, some of them hitting quite close to me, while others hit much farther down the side of the mountain. On one occasion a small mortar shell struck the ground about five or six feet below where I was standing. However, the slope of the hill was so steep, none of the shrapnel from the mortar hit me. My position in relation to the crater dug by the impacting mortar shell was about the same as if I had been standing on a six-foot wall and the shell had hit on the ground beside the wall almost immediately under my feet. After this incident, I continued to dig at a greatly accelerated pace until by the arrival of darkness I was able to assume a reasonably comfortable, crouched position in my foxhole, with two shelter halves stretched over my head to give some protection from the cold, the rain, and the snow.

Late during the night of 4 December, Company C, 135th Infantry, arrived on Mount Pantano and was guided into its previously reconnoitered positions by the platoon sergeants who had accompanied me. We occupied our positions on Mount Pantano from 4 until 8 December. Throughout this period, the Germans shelled us constantly. On several occasions, just before twilight, the shelling was so intense that I was convinced that a determined attack by the Germans in overwhelming force would follow immediately. Although the enemy did not attack, the heavy shell fire killed and wounded many of my men. Moreover, the air was bitterly cold; it rained or snowed almost continually, and a heavy fog hung constantly over the mountain.

By the end of three days, the strength of my entire company was reduced to less than forty men. I seriously doubted the capability of our being able to hold our positions if the Germans should suddenly launch a strong attack immediately after one of their periodic heavy shellings. I immediately contacted the battalion commander and told him of my critical situation, urgently recommending to him that additional men be sent immediately to reinforce my thinly held positions. The much needed help came almost immediately. That same day, before darkness, another rifle company of the 135th Infantry moved into positions in our midst, the new company having a strength of over a hundred men. I now felt that we could repulse the Germans with heavy losses if they should be imprudent enough to attack our sector of Mount Pantano.

During the afternoon of 8 December, one of the heaviest barrages of shell fire I have experienced landed in my company positions. All wire communications were immediately disrupted. The shells were from our own 4.2-inch supporting chemical mortar platoons that, unfortunately for us, had failed to compute the range with sufficient accuracy to permit the shells to clear the crest of the ridge that we occupied and hit as intended, among the Germans on the next ridge. I frantically tried without success to contact the battalion commander by telephone and tell him to contact the 4.2-inch mortar commander and tell him to stop shelling us immediately. I had no better luck contacting my CO by radio. Finally, a volunteer runner succeed in getting through and contacting the battalion commander, who immediately telephoned the 4.2-inch mortar commander. The shelling abruptly ceased, but not before we had suffered heavy casualties.

Late that same afternoon, I received most welcome news that the First Battalion was being relieved from its frontline positions and that, accordingly, I would move my company down the mountain and into a reserve position out of contact with the enemy. A count of my men as I started down the hill disclosed that I had only twenty-eight men left out of an original strength of 185 when I landed in Italy in September. The rest had either been killed, wounded, or fallen prey to disease, trench foot, or psychoneurosis.

On my way to the rear, as I passed Captain Brandt, the battalion executive officer, he surveyed my small force of soldiers in shocked amazement and then asked, "Where is the rest of your company, Captain Bailey? Looks to me like you've got only one squad with you."

We continued marching to the rear until we arrived at a small town, which had not yet received a single round of artillery fire. In utter exhaustion we bedded down on the floor of a large stone house for an anticipated night of sound sleep.

At midnight, I was rudely awakened by the thunderous crash of two heavy enemy shells ripping through the roof of the house adjacent to the one I occupied with the remnant of my company. Evidently the Germans had received word of our presence in town through their superb espionage service. However, in the absence of further shelling, we slept soundly for the remainder of the night.

The next day we moved to the rear several miles to the vicinity of the village of St. Angelo for a few weeks of recuperation, training, reorganization, and resupply.

Chapter XXVIII
Respite from Battle

During the Christmas holiday period of 1943, we rested and trained behind the lines in the vicinity of St. Angelo, Italy. We worked hard physically, but we rested mentally. I think that most of us had almost reached the breaking point under the stress of sustained combat, so we fully enjoyed our brief respite from battle.

On Christmas morning I assembled all of the officers and enlisted men of Company C and read aloud to them from the New Testament, the first fourteen verses of chapter 2 of the Gospel according to St. Luke.

Afterwards we enjoyed a delicious Christmas dinner. The regimental chaplain was our guest. During the meal, he informed me privately that we would soon be returning to the front lines, but that this information was being withheld from the men because of the policy of not taking any action that would spoil their enjoyment of their Christmas dinner. Most of the men of Company C were replacements, recently arrived from the United States. They arrived in St. Angelo and were assigned to my company only about one week before our scheduled return to combat, so I followed the chaplain's advice and decided that I would let them enjoy their Christmas dinner in safety, peace, and quiet while they could.

The day after Christmas we were alerted to move to the front, but we did not leave until 28 December. It was a bitterly cold day with heavily overcast skies and biting wind blowing steadily from the north. We travelled by truck from our area during the afternoon until we arrived shortly before sundown at the base of a low, rocky ridge whose slopes were clad with olive trees. Here we left the trucks and proceeded on foot over a narrow dirt road to the crest of the ridge and thence down the steep slopes of the other side. The road wound in sharp curves toward the broad valley below, past the burned hulks of several American Sherman medium tanks, which were lined up in single file along the road. We trudged past the tanks and through the rubble of the devastated village of San Pietro, which was damaged and shattered beyond any semblance of having ever been a habitable town. In the valley on both sides of the road, there appeared to be what had been at one time beautiful orchards of olive trees. However, that day apparently was no more, as the trunks and branches of the trees had been torn and twisted to shreds by the effects of heavy shell fire. Such a scene of war's ravages, ruin, and desolation I had never seen except in the paintings of Francisco Goya.

We finally arrived at our positions in the front lines shortly after dark so that we were able to relieve a company of the Thirty-sixth Division in place during the hours of darkness. The men of the Thirty-sixth Division told us that their unit had fought several fierce battles in the vicinity of San Pietro and had been able to drive the Germans out of the town after one of their battalions had occupied a steep, rocky peak over a thousand meters in height to our right rear.

On 29 December, I made a long reconnaissance through the hills on our battalion flank and became so completely exhausted I was evacuated to the Seventeenth General Hospital in Naples, where my trouble was diagnosed as yellow jaundice.

Thus began the most pleasant part of my sojourn in Italy. I was taken to the battalion aid station and then I was evacuated by ambulance to the division clearing company where I spent one night. After that I was taken to the Eighth Evacuation Hospital where I spent three days and three nights of complete rest in bed. From there I was taken by train to Naples and placed in the magnificent Seventeenth General Hospital where I lived most comfortably and slept in a soft bed between clean sheets, with no work required of me, and with all the delicious food I could eat until 14 January 1944. I was then released from the hospital and given a two-week period of recuperation at the Naples Replacement Depot, which was located inside a large racetrack.

At the replacement depot I lived in a large pyramidal tent with three other officers. We slept on cots with four blankets. However, the weather was so bitterly cold and damp that we barely managed to keep from freezing. Life at the replacement depot was rather monotonous except that every night we were able to attend a movie or enjoy the personal appearances of famous motion picture stars, such as George Raft or Sterling Holloway.

I remained at the replacement depot until 4 February. Meanwhile, the fighting at Cassino was raging in bitter fury. When I finally arrived at the rear headquarters of the 135th Infantry, I discovered that Captain Garfield now commanded Company C and I was ordered to remain temporarily in the rear area. Except for one or two brief visits to the frontline positions, I did not experience any active combat at that time.

On 8 February the Thirty-fourth Division was relieved from combat duty and moved to St. Angelo.

On 10 February I was assigned as assistant regimental S-3 of the 135th Infantry as the assistant to Capt. Maurice Stacy.

For several days we remained in the St. Angelo area and rested, reorganized, and regrouped for the tasks that we knew still lay ahead of us. Lt. Col. Charles B. Everest of Council Bluffs, Iowa, was temporarily commanding the 135th Infantry Regiment. For over a year he had been our regimental executive officer, serving in this capacity under our highly regarded regimental commander, Col. Robert W. Ward. Prior to January 1943, Colonel Ward had served for several months as the S-3 (plans, training, and operations officer) of the Thirty-fourth Infantry Division, but had gallantly commanded the 135th Infantry through many difficult and terrible actions. Finally, however, he was severely wounded during the bitter fighting at Cassino (which, in its severity and the sustained hardship suffered by all, was the worst period of the war for our regiment) and was evacuated to the Seventeenth General Hospital in Naples for a long, slow period of recuperation. Meanwhile, Lieutenant Colonel Everest assumed command of the 135th Infantry and commanded it with great success and ability during the final phases of the Cassino campaign. The casualties in killed and wounded for the 135th Infantry during the month of January and the first week of February 1943 were the greatest in number of any like period during World War II.

A few days after our arrival in St. Angelo, Lt. Col. Harry W. Sweeting, an armor officer who had formerly commanded a tank battalion with great success in the North African campaign, succeeded Lieutenant Colonel Everest as commanding officer, 135th Infantry, and not long afterwards was promoted to the rank of colonel.

While we were at St. Angelo, our future action remained somewhat obscure. For this reason, this period was called our interim period. We received enough replacements to bring all our units up to full strength; we engaged in basic infantry unit training, emphasizing small tactical exercises and patrol actions; we engaged in some close-order drill to emphasize discipline; we obtained serviceable weapons, equipment, and supplies to replace those lost or destroyed during the Cassino campaign. Our training finally progressed so favorably and so fast that at the end of about two weeks, we were able to have the regiment put on a full-scale review, or parade, with band music. This was a colorful, well-executed affair and did much to make our replacements feel they had finally found a home and belonged to a first-class fighting outfit.

On 4 March, I was placed in charge of an advance party of officers and noncommissioned officers, with representatives from every company in our regiment, and given a mission of moving to the vicinity of the village of Calore for the purpose of setting up,

157

laying out, and organizing an area into which the entire 135th Infantry Regiment would move two days later.

We travelled to our destination without incident, except for rainy, muggy weather. This was a typical small Italian town located among gently rolling hills covered with scattered trees and bushes, some vineyards and some fields of oats and wheat. I selected as our future regimental command post a rather large pink stucco house on the top of a round, gently sloping hill. The house was located outside the limits of Calore and was provided with several smaller outbuildings, also of stucco construction. On one side of the house a reasonably good gravelled road led from the village by the house and into the gentle hills in the valley where the village was situated. Beyond the house was a garden, some vineyards, and a large field of wheat.

I contacted the owner of the pink stucco house, who was an extremely friendly, congenial doctor of perhaps forty years of age. Since he spoke English with a reasonable degree of fluency, I made the mistake of believing that, if we both spoke English, I could understand him and he could understand me well enough for me to accomplish my difficult mission. This was a serious mistake on my part, as subsequent events clearly revealed. I informed him of our immediate requirement of an area in part of his home and his outbuildings as a place to establish our regimental headquarters, and of our larger requirement of an area in the surrounding country large enough to bivouac and use as a training site for an entire infantry regiment of some three thousand men. To my surprise, he agreed readily to my proposals and provided me and the officers with me with the finest accommodations, and the enlisted men with comfortable, dry quarters in the outbuildings in his extensive yard. Also, he treated us with great courtesy and hospitality, giving us some of the finest wine I have ever been privileged to drink in any country, before or since. During the two days I spent in his home prior to the arrival of our regiment, the Italian doctor expressed such friendly feelings for the Americans that I pulled out a photograph of my one-year-old son and showed it to him. He smiled broadly, held up one finger on his right hand, then all fingers on both hands and remarked feelingly, *"Americano, uno bambino; Italiano dieci bambini!"* Since I completely lacked any degree of fluency in Italian, I never quite understood whether the Italian doctor meant that the typical American family had one child, whereas the typical Italian family had ten children; or whether he was trying to tell me he himself had ten children, whereas I had but one child. In any case, it appeared that we were lucky in having at least one warm friend among the Italian people.

During my two-day stay at the doctor's house before our regiment arrived, I was busily engaged in supervising the other members of my advance party in selecting suitable areas to be occupied by each one of the three battalions of our regiment, so that each area would be large enough for a battalion to live in, to train in, and to maneuver in. Additionally, each battalion needed a good road network for its vehicles so they could move freely into and out of the battalion area. Finally, each needed an area with a lot of firm, solid ground on which vehicles could be parked and motor pools could be established. Since the weather was cold and damp with drizzling rain most of the time, we had great difficulty in finding areas that looked good. We were miserable and uncomfortable, and we encountered huge quantities of mud no matter where we went. However, by the afternoon of 5 March, through diligence and persistence we had completed our task, had additionally surveyed the surrounding area with great care, and had selected large areas suitable for general training of the troops of the regiment in large-scale tactical exercises if, and when, such training should be needed.

Late during the morning of 6 March, the remainder of the 135th Infantry arrived and the various battalions were guided into the positions we had selected for them by our advance party representatives. There was some aimless moving around, some vehicles promptly bogged down in the mud, rain fell slowly in a steady drizzle, tempers were short, everyone was cold and miserable, but eventually everyone had either pitched a pup tent, set up a larger tent, or else moved into a suitable building where he could seek shelter from the inclement weather.

The next day we started an intensive training period during which emphasis was placed on the tactics of defense. Heretofore, we had concentrated almost exclusively in training our troops in offensive tactics. Now, however, we emphasized the occupation and organization of defensive positions, reconnaissance patrolling, digging deep foxholes, laying mines, stringing barbwire, training in camouflage, and in several exercises we used indirect fire with our heavy water-cooled Browning machine guns.

Two days after the arrival of the 135th Infantry, my Italian doctor friend sought me out and curtly informed me that his wife was extremely angry because some careless U.S. soldiers had trampled in her garden and damaged her flowers and vegetables, that some of our trucks had shown utter disregard for his rights by leaving the roads and travelling through his field of wheat, and that he personally was greatly disappointed in the rudeness and lack of consideration of the Americans. I, of course, immediately informed my military superiors of the feelings of the Italian doctor and hoped this would end the matter. However, it did not. Moreover, the situation became worse instead of better. My erstwhile Italian friend came to see me for about five successive days, on each visit with the same sad tale: When I first contacted him he had shown such warm hospitality to my men and me, he had no idea that I meant an entire United States regiment of soldiers with some three thousand men and many trucks would move in and literally take over his farm, trample his wheat and his vineyards. He was greatly disappointed in the United States Army. Heretofore, he had considered the American soldiers to be his friends, but it looked like now this friendship couldn't continue any longer. He held me personally accountable for the damage done to his farm because I had been the first American soldier to contact him before the arrival of our regiment. Finally, I became so thoroughly exasperated at this incessant haranguing from the doctor that I reached into my pocket and gave him all the money I had. This amounted to approximately thirty dollars. After that I heard no more from the Italian doctor. Apparently, he was satisfied with my sincerity and regret that I had been responsible for inflicting hardship and trouble on him and his family.

Our training in defense tactics continued smoothly until 21 March, when we were told to prepare to move out immediately to the Anzio beachhead where bitter fighting had been in progress since the early part of January.

The morning of 22 March dawned bright and clear, which put us all in good spirits for our journey to the Anzio beachhead. We boarded trucks and proceeded without incident to the harbor of Naples, almost in the shadow of Mount Vesuvius. While we waited on the beach at Naples to load on the LSTs (small ships), which were to take us to Anzio, I noticed that the crater of Vesuvius, which had been smouldering for several weeks, was now shooting up the greatest, tallest column of thick, white smoke against the azure background of sky that I had ever seen. After resting awhile on the beach and enjoying this awe-inspiring spectacle of Vesuvius, we loaded smoothly aboard our ships late in the afternoon and steamed toward the Anzio beachhead.

Chapter XXIX

Anzio

Most of our journey to Anzio took place during the night, so that our arrival was timed for the next morning, 23 March. This journey was pleasant and uneventful. However, as we pulled slowly into the port of Anzio, two large-caliber enemy shells landed in the water about a hundred yards to our right. We continued to move into the harbor and debarked directly onto the docks. We then loaded hurriedly onto waiting trucks and moved swiftly through the streets of the city and along a paved road across open, flat country for about three miles into a previously selected area, sufficiently large to accommodate all the troops of our regiment. Our chemical warfare troops had placed a multitude of smoke pots around the entire perimeter of the Anzio beachhead to produce such a large volume of smoke that, irrespective of the direction of the wind, it was impossible for the Germans outside our perimeter to observe our movement.

Shortly after our arrival at the regimental assembly area, Colonel Sweeting sent me in a jeep to report to Col. Wiley H. O'MoHundro, commanding officer of the Seventh Infantry Regiment that occupied frontline positions on the defensive perimeter. These positions were centrally located and faced generally north. My mission in visiting the regimental headquarters of the Seventh Infantry was to contact, as quickly as possible, its commander and make the initial arrangements for the 135th Infantry to relieve the Seventh Infantry and occupy their positions. As my jeep moved toward the frontline positions, I noted that the Anzio beachhead had apparently once been a prosperous farming region. Numerous modern stucco houses dotted the countryside, which was flat and covered with luxuriant grass and shade trees. The land was criss-crossed with a checkerboard pattern of well-paved roads running north–south and east–west. I also noted many fat cattle, which had formerly grazed on the rich pastureland, now lying dead on their backs with their feet sticking grotesquely into the air, casualties of the heavy artillery fire the Germans had launched so indiscriminately into our positions. Eventually the bloated and decaying carcasses of the dead cattle created such a horrible stench that the regimental commander was forced to send a detail of a hundred men from frontline duty to bury them.

I noticed that the Mussolini Canal, which was both broad and deep, extended across the entire width of the Anzio perimeter. It formed an excellent secondary line of defense well in rear of our main frontline positions.

Upon approaching within about a hundred yards of Seventh Infantry headquarters, I left my jeep and proceeded the rest of the way on foot. Colonel O'MoHundro's command post was in a concrete house about one mile in rear of the frontline positions. The inside of the house was heavily sandbagged to prevent shattering of its walls under the impact of bursting enemy shells. All movement by vehicle in the vicinity of the house was forbidden during daylight. As soon as I entered the house, I reported to Colonel O'MoHundro and stated my business. He then introduced me to Captain Duncan, his S-3 (plans, training, and operations officer), and to Lieutenant Colonel Toffey, his executive officer. After a short briefing on the enemy and friendly situation, I was invited to accompany the assistant regimental S-3 on a tour of the frontline positions of the Seventh Infantry Regiment in a jeep, this tour to start shortly after dark.

As soon as night fell, we got into a jeep and proceeded to carry out our mission. The night was extremely dark so we had to move very slowly with our lights blacked out completely. First, we proceeded north until our road intersected another road which extended in an east–west direction, generally parallel to, and located only a short distance behind, our front lines. (Perhaps one to two hundred yards is a good estimate.) We turned right on this road and moved deliberately, straining to see something other than the stars. There was no moon to provide any light. All was quiet for the time being, not a shot was being fired by either side. Suddenly the silence of the night was rent by a terrific whistling roar like that of an onrushing tornado. The driver slammed on the brakes with terrific force, bringing his jeep to a sudden halt, which almost unhinged the joints in my neck. All of us jumped, in the twinkling of an eye, and cowered flat in the ditch beside the road as hundreds of flying shell fragments whined over our heads. When silence once more reigned, we rose slowly to our feet and got back in the jeep and proceeded on our way. My host explained that the shells were part of a TOT (time on target) artillery fire plan that the Germans had established by registering their guns on certain road intersections during daylight; then periodically during night hours, they would hurl perhaps thirty shells, more or less, at a single road intersection so that the shells would be timed to arrive on their target at the same instant. In this case, he explained, the Germans were shooting at a road junction just ahead of us. Needless to say, we didn't tarry a single instant at that particular road junction. Soon afterwards we passed one of our own large trucks (two-and-a-half ton) that had been set afire by an enemy shell and was burning fiercely and brilliantly lighting the area for almost a hundred yards around it. We sped quickly past the truck into the outer darkness beyond its circle of light. Altogether we spent several hours that night in our reconnaissance of our friendly positions. We visited the command posts of all of the battalions and several of the company command posts of the Seventh Infantry before returning to the command post of the Seventh Infantry Regiment. All positions we visited were deeply dug in and made extensive use of sandbag barriers in organizing all defensive positions.

ed and the greasy salve smeared over the case. Parts of m
g roll were in shreds and tatters. Had it not been for Captai
n's persuasive invitation to enter the log bunker, I woul
ertainly have been instantly killed during the preceding nigh
he people this incident may be considered as a mere coinci
but to me it has been the most extraordinary and humblin
e that I have ever experienced or ever heard of anyone els
encing.

ill badly shaken by my narrow escape from death, I reporte
Sweeting for orders on 15 May. He immediately told me
report to the command post of the First Battalion to replac
Arnold Brandt, who was to return to the U.S.A. on rotatio
job was to be that of battalion executive officer to Lt. Co
Phelan, who had recently assumed command of the Fir
on. At this time, the First Battalion, along with the rest of th
nt, was engaged in intensive preparations to launch a ma
tack to be closely coordinated with elements of the Fir
ed Division in what was called Plan Buffalo. The objectiv
a Buffalo was to break out of the Anzio beachhead, mov
north, and capture the city of Rome.

he First Battalion was at this time in division reserve in a re
veral thousand yards behind the front lines. It was planne
r the attack our battalion would be attached to Comb
and A of the First Armored Division and that from the ve
ing of the attack infantrymen and armor troops would mo
unit, operating closely in a coordinated, massive infantr
am. The attack was to be led by a wave of medium tanks th
push before them a long steel "snake" loaded througho
th with high explosives, which were to detonate the midd
minefield the Germans had laid in front of their positio
h this breach, closely following the tanks, our infantrym
pour through and overwhelm the enemy before they cou
r from the shock of being attacked by the tanks. Immediate
the infantrymen a wave of light tanks was to follow for t

I remained the rest of the night and all the next day at the command post of the Seventh Infantry, gaining as much familiarity as I could with the overall scheme of defense and the location of positions, as well as the current plans for counterattack in case any of our positions should be overrun by the enemy. The next afternoon, Colonel Sweeting and a small number of his key staff officers arrived in the command post (CP) and that night the 135th Infantry Regiment replaced the Seventh Infantry in all of its positions and thereafter assumed responsibility for defending this sector of the Anzio beachhead perimeter. The relief of one regiment by the other proceeded smoothly and was executed without the enemy discovering that the relief was in progress.

For a few days, I remained at headquarters, 135th Infantry Regiment, and carried out my duties as assistant regimental S-3 as assistant to Maj. Donald Landon, who had formerly commanded Company A. However, unexpectedly I was detailed to duty as an instructor in the Thirty-fourth Division Battle School, which had been established in a large wooded rear area by Lt. Col. Charles P. Greyer, a recently assigned officer. Lieutenant Colonel Greyer had established his school in a large clearing in the forest, which was the site of a small Italian village of mud huts and thatched roofs. The Italians had been evacuated from the houses several days before and hence they were not present to hinder us in conducting our training.

The mission of our battle school was to provide an intensive three-day course of battle instruction in scouting and patrolling; small unit tactics; and in the specialized techniques of pillbox reduction, and street and village fighting. Since many of the members of the Thirty-fourth Division were relatively untrained replacements, Major General Ryder had directed the establishment of the Thirty-fourth Division Battle School to insure that all these replacements would get the opportunity to receive training in special battle techniques from combat-hardened veterans. Each group of students reported to our school and spent three days receiving our instruction, then returned to its unit, in turn to be replaced by another group of students. The size of groups was small, not exceeding forty to fifty men.

The sleeping quarters for both our faculty and students were located in heavy log bunkers with thick overhead cover of logs and dirt. We were thus relatively safe from attack or shell fire, so much so that our school provided a welcome rest period where our students could relax after the strain of constant danger experienced in the front lines.

My job in the school was to give practical instruction in street and village fighting. This we accomplished through using several of the buildings in the Italian village. Also, I gave instruction in scouting and patrolling, wherein all students were given a mission and required to execute it at night in a previously laid out area we had designated in the woods.

Throughout most of April and the first two weeks of May, our battle school continued to fulfill its mission of instructing large numbers of Thirty-fourth Division infantrymen in battle tactics. Usually, everything went smoothly. Classes were held on schedule, and, periodically, the German "Anzio Express" shells would roar over our heads on their way from the German gunners to targets somewhere in the harbor of Anzio.

On 14 May, we received word to suspend further operations of our battle school and report back to our respective units to assist in preparing to launch a major attack against the Germans. In accordance with these instructions, I loaded my heavy bedding roll on a jeep and reported late during the afternoon of 14 May to headquarters, 135th Infantry Regiment, near the Mussolini Canal. I was told to remain at regimental headquarters until the next day when I would receive information concerning my new assignment. Meanwhile, I was told to relax and to make myself comfortable for the night.

Since it was a beautiful evening with brilliant moonlight, bright stars in the sky and a soft, gentle breeze blowing, I decided

that I would sleep in the open air rather than
large log bunkers that covered the area. Accor
bedding and spread it out on the ground b
occupied by Capt. Wilhelm M. Johnson, ou
and two or three other regimental staff offic
noted my actions and invited me to move in
there was still plenty of room. I thanked him
him I had slept so may nights in damp dug
outside and enjoy some of the sweet-smelli
proceeded to lie down in my bedroll and had
when Captain Johnson came outside and aga
inside the bunker and sleep. For the secon
politely, but refused to move inside the bu
empty canvas cot reserved for me. A few mi
had almost fallen asleep, Captain Johnson c
for the third time and urged me to reconside
on the ground outside the bunker. I replied th
as to invite me for the third time to move insi
be a rude person if I didn't move inside imi
was with some reluctance that I finally mo
and slept on a cot for the rest of the night
meanwhile leaving my bedroll spread out c
side.

Suddenly, at about midnight, I was a
crashing roar of exploding bombs just outs
sharp pungent odor of burnt cordite wafted t
morning, upon going outside the bunker, I
the night a low-flying German plane had ci
had dropped several small antipersonnel bo
log bunkers. One of these bombs scored a d
roll, ripping several large holes and ma
blankets, in the canvas cover of my bedding
map case I had left on top of my bedding ro
a bottle of Vicks salve, which I carried

purpose of mopping up and knocking out machine-gun nests. Our troops were to keep moving forward to objectives approximately four thousand yards ahead of the then existing frontline positions, then halt, dig in, and wait for the Thirty-sixth Infantry Division on our right to capture the city of Velletri, and then swing abreast of us to continue the attack.

For several days, we trained with the troops of the First Armored Division, practicing the unfamiliar coordinating tactical exercises with tanks. Meanwhile, every night the Allied artillery weapons from all parts of the Anzio perimeter laid down a heavy and sustained artillery barrage into the German positions to deceive our enemy as to the date and time of our scheduled attack.

Finally, during the afternoon of 23 May, all the field grade officers and acting field grade officers of the First Armored and Thirty-fourth Divisions assembled at the headquarters of the First Armored Division for a detailed briefing by Maj. Gen. Ernest N. Harmon, commanding general, First Armored Division. We assembled round a huge sand table that showed in bold relief and in almost exact detail the main terrain features of the Anzio beachhead and of the various troop dispositions of all our units and the German units. It was a clear day and the sun was already sinking low toward the horizon in the west. In a never-to-be-forgotten briefing, Major General Harmon held a long pointer in his hands and explained what he expected each battalion to accomplish the next morning just before daylight, which was to be the time of our attack. Then he paused in the midst of his briefing, glanced briefly toward the setting sun and remarked earnestly, "Gentlemen, you all see that the sun is now about to set. Take a good look at it. Many of us here present today will no doubt bite the dust ere the sun sinks from view tomorrow. But in spite of that fact we are going to attack the Germans tomorrow morning, and by G——, we're going to *win*."

With this final dramatic statement, the meeting broke up and we returned to our units, issued detailed instructions to our men, then went to bed.

At 0200 hours on 24 May, we moved slowly toward the front lines, which were then occupied by another unit. The night was pitch-black, so the men were required to wear small round phosphorescent "cats' eyes" on the rear of their helmets as a guide to the troops immediately behind them so they could tell the direction of travel. Because of the deep darkness, men had to follow closely behind one another or else be separated and lost. This also applied to our vehicles. Thus when we got underway, we were strung out in a long, closely packed column of men, jeeps, and trucks, moving straight forward along a road leading directly to the frontline positions. It was the dark of the moon, so visibility was practically zero. Luckily for us, during the entire movement forward, not a single round of German artillery or mortar fire landed among us. If our movement had been known to the Germans, we were in a position to suffer terrible casualties. With this good luck, however, our troops were in their attack positions long before the appointed hour of dawn. I did not accompany our troops all the way forward to the front, since, in my capacity as battalion executive officer, I had to remain at the battalion command post. Accordingly, with my small group of battalion headquarters personnel, I fell out of the column and remained at my CP position next to my telephone.

Promptly at dawn on 24 May, behind a heavy artillery barrage, our troops surged furiously forward. Initially the attack of our troops encountered bitter resistance, but it soon gathered momentum and rolled rapidly forward against the shocked, surprised German defenders. Encouraged by the gallant example of their junior leaders, our troops continued to rush forward with a burst of impregnable fury and sent such a hail of machine-gun and small arms fire into the ranks of the enemy that they could not hold their positions. Many of the Germans surrendered without much of a fight. Meanwhile, the impetus of the attack of Combat Command A continued to roll forward far beyond our originally assigned objectives. In this manner, the attack continued with uninterrupted success for about three days. On one dark night, I was talking on the phone to the regimental commander, who asked me to relay some information to the battalion commander. I told him I had lost contact with the battalion commander. The regimental commander then ordered me to move up to the battalion observation post and assume command of the battalion and continue the attack at dawn.

It was already only about two hours until daylight, so I stumbled hurriedly forward, contacted all the company commanders of the First Battalion, issued my attack order, and was all set to move out. Meanwhile it was almost time to cross the line of departure. Suddenly, the battalion commander appeared from seemingly nowhere (he had been fast asleep on the floor of a nearby house) and demanded, "What the h——l is going on here, anyhow?" When I told him why I was there, he told me he had been so exhausted the night before that he had gone to bed early and slept until a few minutes ago. He then told me to return to the battalion command post and he would direct the continued attack of our battalion. Without further argument or discussion, I returned to the command post.

Meanwhile, the First Battalion attack continued until it encountered extremely heavy resistance at Lanuvio, on 29 May. Our attack was stopped cold and during the next two or three days we received some of the most intensive shelling I had ever seen.

Finally, on 3 June, our troops launched an attack before dawn that gradually gained momentum and carried forward all the way to the main road leading to Rome. At this time, our infantry troops were riding on the tanks and the attack was proceeding with extreme rapidity. As battalion executive officer, I remained at the battalion command post and was in contact with Lieutenant Colonel Phelan only by radio. The movement was now proceeding so rapidly that I was so far behind I could hear his voice only with great difficulty. Finally, I understood that he wanted me to form the battalion vehicles into a rear echelon group and try to catch up as soon as possible with the main body. As quickly as possible, I started the execution of this order.

Later, as my jeep entered a main road intersection on the road to Rome, as far as I could see in both directions from right and left there were two interminably long columns of American tanks and other assorted vehicles moving toward Rome. On top of a steep bank on the far side of a road junction, with his rifle clutched tightly in his hand, sat a dead German soldier with a black, bloated, rapidly decomposing face. He was propped crazily in a sitting position against the steep bank of the road junction. Although he and his brave comrades had fought bravely and bitterly to the last, they and he with his lone rifle had not been equal to the task of stopping the advance of the Thirty-fourth Infantry and First Armored Divisions, now moving so relentlessly in pursuit of the fast-retreating German army.

Chapter XXX

Pursuit

Late during the afternoon of 4 June, we entered Rome, the Eternal City, which the Germans had evacuated in such haste they neglected to destroy the buildings in Rome and the bridges across the Tiber River. The Romans were overwhelmed with joy at our entry into their city. They yelled with a deafening roar, surged round us, and tossed bouquets of flowers at us from all directions. Hundreds of pretty girls swarmed into our jeeps, threw their arms round our dirty necks and bearded, unkempt faces, and hugged and kissed us passionately. Our progress was thus delayed and we did not reach the Colosseum, our prearranged assembly area, until twilight.

Finally, I entered a building where our battalion command post was located temporarily, took off my heavy gear, and prepared to lie down to sleep. Meanwhile, Lieutenant Colonel Phelan contacted me and told me he had an important mission for me. He wanted me to visit each bridge across the Tiber River and personally check to see that his orders had been carried out to place a platoon of infantry and a platoon of tanks at each bridge site to prevent the Germans from returning to recapture or destroy the bridge. I immediately commandeered the services of a local civilian and an Italian-speaking American soldier, plus a jeep driver. We all loaded into my jeep and set out through the darkness for the bridges across the Tiber River. It took me the remainder of the night to visit each bridge, but I carried out my orders faithfully and found all bridges well guarded and encountered no snipers along the way. I finally returned to my sleeping quarters just before dawn and flopped wearily into my bedding roll.

Shortly thereafter, Col. Sweeting visited our command post and told us to get ready to move out immediately in pursuit of the Germans who were reportedly fleeting precipitately northward. Shortly after dawn, we resumed our rapid advance after the fleeting German army. Our impetuous regimental commander, ever in the vanguard of his troops, got too far in the lead and was suddenly cut off and captured.

While this rapid action was taking place and before I had learned what had happened to Colonel Sweeting, the commanding general of Combat Command A espied me, got out of his jeep, and told me he wanted to talk to Lieutenant Colonel Phelan. I replied that I was unable to contact him by radio and wasn't exactly sure of his whereabouts. Next he asked me to contact the regimental commander by radio. Since I couldn't do this either—because (unknown to me) Colonel Sweeting had just been captured by the Germans—the general angrily made some caustic comments about wasting his time trying to get vitally needed information from an infantry battalion executive officer who didn't know where either his battalion commander or his regimental commander was. With these parting words, he jumped into his jeep again and continued his rapid movement to the head of the column of tanks.

Shortly thereafter, when we learned what had happened to Colonel Sweeting, Lt. Col. Charles P. Greyer, the regimental executive officer, assumed command of the 135th Infantry; and we continued our pursuit of the retreating German army.

All along the way, large numbers of dead horses, which the Germans in Italy were still using to pull their artillery and wagons, littered the roadsides. The horses had been killed by our bombing attacks. We continued our pursuit of the Germans for several days until finally we arrived at the city of Viterbo on 9 June, when we were relieved and moved to the little village of Saline on the

174

seacoast near Civitavecchia. We remained at this location until 26 June and engaged in rigorous training exercises.

While we were at Saline, Lt. Col. Ashton Manhart assumed command of the 135th Infantry and was promoted to the grade of colonel not long afterwards.

On 26 June we went back into action but did not engage in any heavy fighting until 2 July. On that date we commenced a bitter engagement that lasted until 5 July. We were no longer pursuing the Germans. They had now definitely taken a firm stand and were bitterly contesting every foot of our advance.

During this period of bitter fighting, it was often difficult to keep proper contact with all the frontline elements and to keep them fully supplied with ammunition and hot meals at night. Because of the heavy fire received from the Germans, our vehicles could move in forward areas only after nightfall.

On all except one occasion, we were successful in getting a hot meal forward to feed the troops shortly after darkness. On this occasion the guides got lost and couldn't make contact with our fighting elements. I got into the act myself and we wandered aimlessly all night long and never did make contact with our frontline companies. Finally when dawn broke, I was astonished to see our front lines about fifty feet away from me on the other side of a little creek with thick bushes and undergrowth along its sides. On another occasion the jeeps were loaded with the food containers to feed the troops a hot meal when the mess personnel came to me and told me they were afraid to travel over the road ahead of them because somebody told them it had antitank mines in it. I jumped into the lead jeep and proceeded without incident up to the front lines. The other jeeps followed me closely. We didn't run over any mines.

On 4 July, our battalion was subjected to heavy shell fire throughout the day. We had plenty of fireworks through the courtesy of the Germans. Our joint command-observation post was located in a large stone house at the base of a low ridge on which were located our front lines. Suddenly an old lady, who had been concealed in the house, approached me wringing her hands and crying pitifully. I asked her through an Italian-speaking soldier what she was crying about. She replied this was her house and the American soldiers had killed all her chickens but one, and now they were trying to catch that one also. I immediately looked out into the yard and sure enough a fleet-footed U.S. soldier was pursuing an even fleeter-footed chicken, which was running around in a circle. Meanwhile, shells were hitting sporadically in the general vicinity; none of them had yet hit the house. I went into the yard and sternly ordered the soldier to quit chasing the chicken. And furthermore I told him that if I saw him or anyone else eating the old lady's chickens, I would immediately send them to the front lines to see if they could chase Germans as fast as they could chase a chicken.

We continued our bitter fighting until 14 July.

In order to maintain contact with the battalion commander and our frontline units, I tried to spend a part of each day at the observation post with the battalion commander and the rest of the day at the command post.

On one of the days during this period, our attacking troops had advanced rapidly and were now located on a ridge several hundred yards ahead of where I was. Shortly before sunset, I set out for the frontline positions. When I approached the front line, I noticed some men dug in along a hedge. They pointed to a house on the crest of the ridge and told me Lieutenant Colonel Phelan was inside the house. There were several outside steps leading from the ground into the second floor of the house. I ran up the steps and gained the cover of the building to avoid sniper fire, which I was told had been hitting the house all during the afternoon. Inside the house Lieutenant Colonel Phelan was manning a light machine gun and looking out the upstairs window toward the German positions on a parallel ridge only a few hundred yards away. Captain Windsor, commanding officer of Company A, was looking out another window, also manning a machine gun.

Suddenly Lieutenant Colonel Phelan yelled, "Look out, here they come!"

Immediately the air was rent by the thunderous roar of our troops firing machine guns and rifles at the onrushing Germans who had just launched a counterattack in our direction. This heavy fire stopped the Germans who slowly fell back to their previous positions. It had been a brief, bitter action, but the German counterattack had failed.

A few days later on 14 July, as we were advancing through the village of Rosignano, I suddenly received orders to report with all my baggage and equipment to the regimental headquarters.

Chapter XXXI
Rotation

I rode slowly toward the headquarters of the 135th Infantry in a jeep. As I rode, I pondered the possible reasons for being ordered to leave the First Battalion. I was somewhat disappointed at not being permitted to remain in the position of infantry battalion executive officer long enough to be promoted to the grade of major. However, I realized that in one respect I had been extremely fortunate, even though I hadn't been promoted to major. After all, I was still alive and I had never been wounded. I was one of seven officers left in the 135th Infantry Regiment out of an original number of approximately 130 officers who had departed from New York almost twenty-seven months ago aboard the *Aquitania*. Of these seven officers still left in the 135th Infantry, five were dentists, doctors, and chaplains, who had not been subjected to the full fury of infantry combat for the total period of time in which the 135th Infantry had been in action.

Shortly after my arrival at regimental headquarters, Colonel Manhart told me he believed that I had seen enough combat action for this war, that he had designated Maj. James E. Tyler to succeed me as First Battalion executive officer, and that I was scheduled to return to the United States on rotation in a few weeks. Meanwhile, I had been designated as commanding officer of the regimental replacement company. I remained in this job until 26 July, all the while supervising a hard, rugged program of bayonet training, small unit tactical exercises, and long marches with full field packs to whip the new replacements quickly into shape to fight.

On 26 July, I moved to Thirty-fourth Division Headquarters where I was assigned comfortable quarters in a tent until 30 July. On that date I proceeded in company with many other happy officers and men to the port of Piombino. From thence we went aboard a Liberty ship and sailed to Naples where we remained in large, comfortable pyramidal tents in the Naples Replacement Depot until 16 August.

On 16 August, I boarded the U.S. Army transport ship *General Black* and embarked for the United States. I was given command of four hundred men on the ship and continually harassed and hounded about dirty latrines, improperly made beds, unswept decks, etc. Nevertheless, it was the most delightful voyage I have ever taken.

We were served excellent meals every day that included delicious white bread and real butter.

On the night of 31 August, we arrived in New York Harbor, but we remained on board the ship until the next morning. We were surprised to see so many automobiles running along the highways in the U.S.A. as we thought that rationing was so severe that one couldn't run an automobile for any purpose.

On 1 September 1944, I finally marched down the gangplank of the *General Black* and set foot once more on the soil of the U.S.A. after an absence of twenty-eight months and two days. Several pretty Red Cross girls were standing at the gangplank to welcome us home by giving each of us a free bottle of milk.

Epilogue

Within one hour after my arrival at the port of embarkation in New York City, I was completely processed and on my way by train to Fort Bragg, near Fayetteville, North Carolina, where I arrived during the late afternoon of 1 September.

After spending the night at Fort Bragg, I was granted a two-week leave of absence. I immediately boarded a Trailways bus for a 150-mile ride to a joyous reunion with my wife, Sarah, at her home in Williamston, North Carolina, and for a first meeting with my nineteen-month-old son, Leslie W. Bailey, Jr., whom I had never seen.

One of my happiest memories of our first day together was going for a ride in our 1941 Chevrolet automobile, with me driving and our son standing between Sarah and me. He apparently realized that I had not driven a car lately as he kept commenting every time we met another automobile, "Cah comin', cah comin'."

During our ride Sarah told me she had written a letter to me every single day during our twenty-eight months of separation. However, mail delivery overseas was so uncertain that I sometimes did not receive a letter from her for two to three weeks at a time; then I would receive fifteen or twenty of her letters on a single day.

Sarah and I had been married since 1 March 1942, shortly after my arrival at Fort Dix, New Jersey, in February of that year. Because of our alert status at that time and my impending journey overseas, we had never had the opportunity to take a honeymoon.

However, the joy of our reunion was complete when at the end of my all-too-short leave of absence, we learned that when the U.S. Army acts, it acts swiftly, compassionately, and in a grand manner.

To our surprise, Sarah and I were assigned to a period of two weeks of rest, rehabilitation, and relaxation in one of the finest rooms of one of the most luxurious hotels on Collins Avenue in a beautiful southern city on the Atlantic Coast. We were charged $1.50 per day for a spacious double room. So, after twenty-eight long months of separation and successfully passing through hell and high water separately, we were together at last for our glorious honeymoon in Miami Beach, Florida.

Appendices

Appendix A

Field Order for Attack of Third Battalion, 135th Infantry, on Harbor of Algiers, North Africa, on Morning of 8 November 1942

UNITED STATES TERMINAL FORCE
OPERATION TERMINAL

FO 1
MAPS: "*Deleted*": AUG. '42 1:12:00

1.
- a. Situation
  (See Intelligence Summary Appendix I) [not included in this book]
- b. *FORCES AVAILABLE*
  - (a) three Rifle Companies plus one Platoon Hvy MG plus Section 81mm Mortars.
  - (b) two Destroyers (BROKE and MALCOLM).
  - (c) Naval Boarding Party, 60 Officers and Men.
  - (d) Naval Intelligence Party, One Officer and six men.

2. *MISSION:*
To prevent sabotage of port facilities and the scuttling of ships in the port of———.

3.
- a. *PLAN A*
  BROKE will lead into the basin de MUSTAPHA thru the

Southern entrance with the MALCOLM one mile astern. It is the intention to strike the boom between No. 7 and No. 8 lighters counting from the BRISE LAMES EST. BROKE will endeavor to berth alongside QUAI DE DIEPPE. MALCOLM will follow in and berth ALONGSIDE GRAND MOLE, QUAI DE CETTE.

b. 1st Phase, Plan A:

Predicated on both destroyers berthing at points planned above, Company L is to seize objectives A, B, and C, as shown on the map, and secure all entrances through the guard fence from Point G2 to a point opposite QUAI DE DIEPPE.

Company K to seize objectives D, E, F, and the PORT OFFICES, also to secure entrances to dock area along guard fence from point opposite the QUAI DE DIEPPE to the PORT OFFICES.

Company I plus 1st PLATOON Heavy Machine Guns and 1 Section 81 mm Mortars to assemble at the root of GRAND MOLE to constitute FORCE RESERVE.

c. Plans B and C

Predicated upon the failure of one of the destroyers in which case the other one is to seize all the objectives assigned to both of them.

d. 2nd Phase Plan A

On completion of Phase I about first light it is intended to press on to VIEUX PORT leaving sufficient forces to contain objectives gained. Other troops landing on B beach will move towards ILOT DE LA MARINE. It is intended to join up with these forces for an assault on MARINE OFFICES.

4. Two units of fire will be unloaded from destroyers and location of Ammunition Distributing Point issued later.

Reserve rations and packs to be left on board destroyers until the situation has clarified.

5. Under PLAN A or PLAN B the Force Command Post will be located at the root of the GRAND MOLE. Under PLAN C, the initial Command Post will be at the QUAI DE DAKAR; as the plan progresses, the Command Post will be moved to the root of the GRAND MOLE.

For Code see Appendix 2 (NOT GIVEN, CODE NOT AVAILABLE).

For recognition information to be passed to all members, see Appendix 3 (NOT GIVEN—UNAVAILABLE).

Appendix B

Field Order for Attack of Company K (Reinforced), 135th Infantry (Malcolm Group), on Harbor of Algiers, North Africa, on Morning of 8 November 1942

1. *FORCES AVAILABLE*
    a. Company K.
    b. $\frac{1}{2}$ of Company I, including $\frac{1}{2}$ of all available weapons.
2. *MISSION:*
    To prevent sabotage of port facilities and to seize and secure objectives D, E, F, and PORT OFFICES and to prevent any enemy forces from moving into the dock area by securing all entrances from G1 NORTH of PORT OFFICES, SOUTH to a line running WEST from QUAI DE DIEPPE.
3. *DETAILED PLAN*
    COMPANY K
    a. FIRST PLATOON COMPANY K commanded by Lt. VOSS, will move rapidly along line G1 to CO. K, Co. L boundary line (running WEST from QUAI DE DIEPPE) securing all entrances to dock area and will prevent any enemy forces from entering the dock area.
    b. SECOND PLATOON COMPANY K commanded by Lt. BAILEY, will seize and secure PORT OFFICES AND OBJECTIVE F, and will prevent sabotage to those port

facilities. Lt. BAILEY with two RIFLE SQUADS and one BROWNING AUTOMATIC RIFLE (BAR) TEAM will move to PORT OFFICES. STAFF SERGEANT HILL with one RIFLE SQUAD and one BAR TEAM will move to MOLE AL MOUCHEZ.

c. THIRD PLATOON COMPANY K commanded by Lt. FLYNN, will seize and secure objectives D, E, and will prevent sabotage to these Port Facilities (Lt. FLYNN with two RIFLE SQUADS and one BAR TEAM at GRAND MOLE; STAFF SERGEANT TROTTER with one RIFLE SQUAD and one BAR TEAM at MOLE AUX MINERAIS).

d. WEAPONS PLATOON COMPANY K, commanded by Lt. DOTY will remain in vicinity of Company COMMAND POST until employed by COMPANY COMMANDER.

e. Immediately upon securing objectives, SECOND and THIRD PLATOONS will reinforce line formed by FIRST PLATOON.

f. One half of COMPANY I will be in RESERVE along QUAI DE BREST.

4. Ammunition Distributing Point will be at QUAI DE CETTE on Board DESTROYER MALCOLM until action moves forward. Medical Aid will be supplied by attached First Aid Men, one per RIFLE PLATOON. "C" Ration will be eaten only upon the order of an officer.

5. COMPANY COMMAND POST will be a root of even AUX MINERAIS. I will be at OBSERVATION POST on RAMP CHASSERIAU, at point on line extending EAST from QUAI DE BORDEAUX.

Appendix C

Maps of Landing Operations in North Africa on November 8, 1942

Map A. The Allied Invasion General Map
Map B. Allied Landings in Algiers Area 8 November 1942
Map C. The Attack on Algiers Harbor 8 November 1942

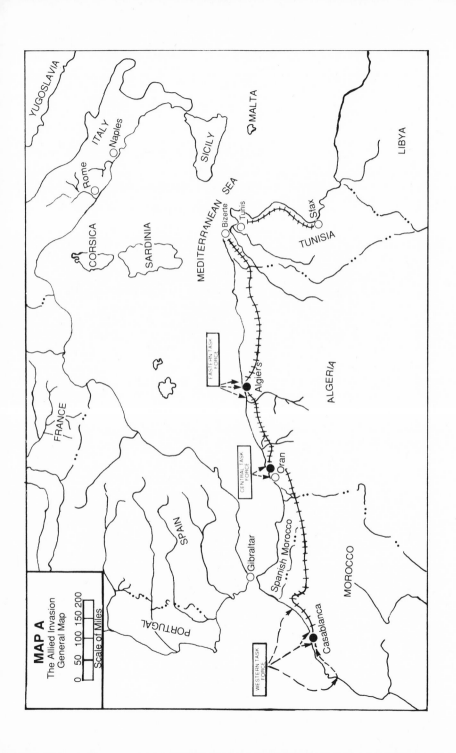

MAP A
The Allied Invasion
General Map

Scale of Miles
0 50 100 150 200

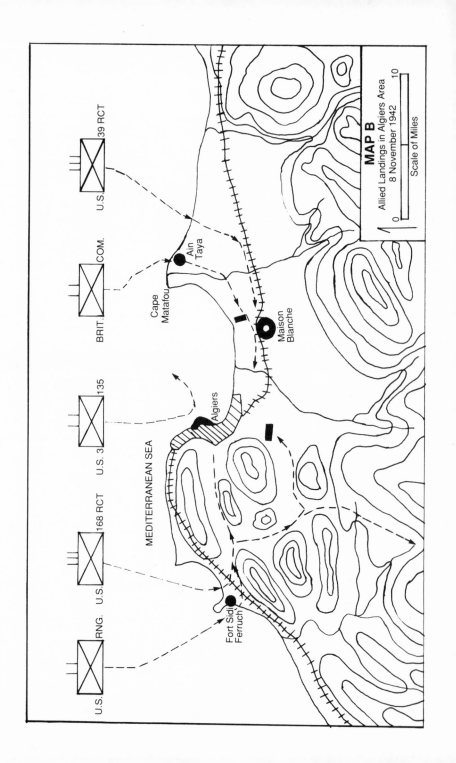

MAP B

Allied Landings in Algiers Area
8 November 1942

Scale of Miles
0   10

MEDITERRANEAN SEA

U.S. RNG.   U.S. 168 RCT   U.S. 3 135   BRIT. COM.   U.S. 39 RCT

Fort Sidi Ferruch

Algiers

Cape Matafou

Ain Taya

Maison Blanche

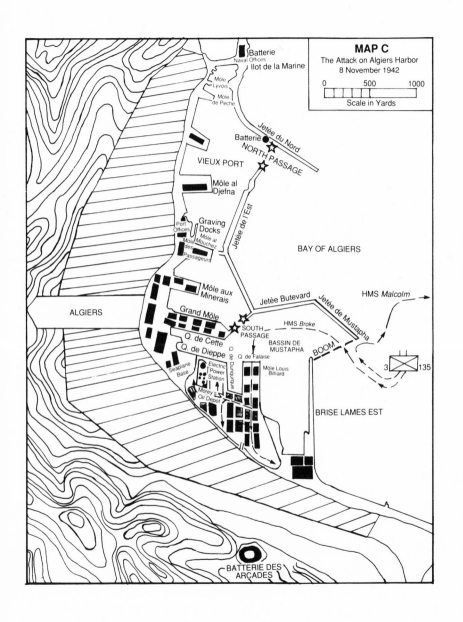

MAP C

The Attack on Algiers Harbor
8 November 1942

0   500   1000
Scale in Yards

Batterie
Naval Offices
Ilot de la Marine
Mòle Lyvois
Mòle de Peche

Jetée du Nord
Batterie
NORTH PASSAGE

VIEUX PORT

Mòle al Djefna

Jetée de l'Est

BAY OF ALGIERS

Port Offices
Graving Docks
Mòle al Mouchez
Mòle des Passageurs

Mòle aux Minerais

Jetée Butevard   Jetée de Mustapha

HMS Malcolm

Grand Mòle

ALGIERS

SOUTH PASSAGE
HMS Broke

Q. de Cette
Q. de Dieppe

BASSIN DE MUSTAPHA

BOOM

3   135

Seaplane Base
Electric Power Station
Q. de Dunqurque
Q. de Falaise
Mòle Louis Billiard

Morey's Oil Depot

BRISE LAMES EST

BATTERIE DES ARCADES

Index

Abercorn, Duke of, 24

Afrika Korps, 88, 93

Ain-El-Turk, North Africa, 128

Alexander, Harold, British general, 86, 104

Algiers, North Africa, 39, 41–43, 47, 49, 52, 54, 56–57, 61–63, 65–66, 70–71, 86, 116, 122, 124, 185, 188, 190–93

Alife, Italy, 137

Amorisi, Italy, 135

Anderson, First Lieutenant, 68

Anderson, K. A. N., British general, 41

Anderson, Roland, Maj., 122, 125

Anzio beachhead, 161–62, 165, 168

Appleton, Minnesota, 67

Aquitania, British transport ship, 8, 11, 12

Argyle, Duke of, 26, 27

Ashbrooke, Northern Ireland, 21

Atkinson, Second Lieutenant, 126

Baer, Lieutenant Colonel, 26

Bailey, Leslie W., Jr., 84, 181

Bailey, Sarah H., 4, 6–8, 84, 181–82

Ballycastle, Northern Ireland, 15, 17

Béja, North Africa, 101

Belfast, Northern Ireland, 31–34

Bell, battalion chaplain, 17, 97

Bell, Gail R., First Lieutenant, 68, 126, 135, 143, 149

Bizerte, North Africa, 57, 65, 116–17

Boston, Massachusetts, 67

Bovain, Second Lieutenant, 67

Bradford, Sergeant, 31

Bradley, Omar N., Lt. Gen., 104–5

Brandt, Arnold N., 1st Lt., Capt., Maj., 67–68, 74, 79, 112–13, 152, 168

Broke, HMS, destroyer, British navy, 31–32, 35, 37–38, 42–48, 55

Bulolo, headquarters ship, Eastern Task Force, 27, 52

Caffey, Benjamin, Brig, Gen., 121

Camp Blessingbourne, Northern Ireland, 30

Camp Claiborne, Louisiana, 2

Casablanca, North Africa, 41, 116

Cashman, Father, chaplain, 68

Cassino, Italy, 156–57

Chegin, Tom, 1st Lt., 31, 60

Chouigui Pass, North Africa, 113, 115, 118

Chouigui village, North Africa, 115, 121

Churchill, Lt. Col., British Army officer, 27, 28

Churchill, Randolph, Capt., British army officer, 52

Churchill, Winston, British prime minister, 39

Civitavecchia, Italy, 175

Clairfontaine, North Africa, 86

Colebrook, Northern Ireland, 21, 31

Colosseum, Rome, Italy, 173

Council Bluffs, Iowa, 156

Crocker, John, Lt. Gen., British army, 100

de Gaulle, Charles, French general, 127

Djebel Trozzia, North Africa, 76, 82, 85, 92

Dodge, First Lieutenant, 99

Donora, Pennsylvania, 60

Doty, Luther L., 2nd Lt., 31, 38, 59–60, 189

Dragoni, Italian town, 136

Drake, Lieutenant Colonel, 24

Drury, Second Lieutenant, 117

Duncan, Captain, 163

Dungannon, Northern Ireland, 22

Eddekehila, North Africa, 112, 115, 118

Eisenhower, Dwight D., Lt. Gen., Gen., 41, 104–5, 111, 119

El Rhorab, North Africa, 87–89, 94

Ely Lodge, Northern Ireland, 30

Erikson, Ray, Capt., Maj., 122, 145

Everest, Charles B, Lt. Col., 156–57

Exercise Atlantic, 21

Fancourt, Captain, British navy, 34, 36, 43–45, 47, 55

Fanning, Charles, Capt., 68, 78, 106, 126

Flynn, John W., 2nd Lt., 31, 38, 59–60, 189

Fondouk, North Africa, 17, 85–88, 92, 96–99

Fort Bragg, North Carolina, 1, 181

Fort Dix, New Jersey, 1–2, 6–8, 10

Fotakis, Second Lieutenant, 67, 93

Fredendall, Lloyd, Maj. Gen., 41

Garfield, Captain, 156

General Black, U.S. Liberty ship, 179

Gettysburg, Pennsylvania, 53, 89

Gibraltar, 34, 39

Giraud, Henri, French general, 119, 127

Glover, Ivan L., Sgt., 126, 148

Gould, Second Lieutenant, 68

Greenwood, Julian L., Sgt., 126

Greller, First Lieutenant, 26

Greyer, Charles P., Lt. Col., 165, 174

Halifax, Nova Scotia, 12

Hall, Garnett, Maj., 68

Hamblin, Captain, battalion surgeon, 68

Harmon, Ernest N., Maj. Gen., 169

Henley, Second Lieutenant, 68–69, 71, 117

Hill, Staff Sergeant, 189

Hill 609 (Djebel Tahent), 102–3, 111

Hitler, Adolf, German dictator, 6, 104, 128

Holloway, Sterling, 156

Huguette, nine-year-old French girl, 60, 62–63, 65

Inveraray, Scotland, 25–26

Jackson, Andrew, general in War of 1812, 100

Johnson, Second Lieutenant, 134

Johnson Wilhelm M., Capt., regimental surgeon, 32, 167–68

Jolson, Al, 17

Kairouan, North Africa, 75, 78, 87

Kanstrup, Arthur A., Capt., 1

Kasbah, Algiers, 57–58, 61

Kasserine Pass, North Africa, 81, 83

Kesselring, Albert, Field Marshal, German army in Italy, 128

Kipling, Rudyard, 119

Koulgeorge, Second Lieutenant, 68

Landon, Donald C., Capt., Maj., 68, 106, 122, 165

Lanuvio, Italy, 171

Layard, Commander, British navy, 43, 45, 55

L'Ecole de Jeune Filles, 60, 65

Le Kef, North Africa, 76, 85

Lillo, Mr. and Mrs., French hosts, 63–64

Lindstrand, Second Lieutenant, 126

Londonderry, Northern Ireland, 14

Lyons, John, 1st Lt., 26, 63, 68, 134, 140

Macktar Forest, North Africa, 73, 76, 99

Malcolm, HMS, destroyer, British navy, 31–32, 35, 37–38, 42–45, 50–53

Maness, Second Lieutenant, 126

Manhart, Ashton, Lt. Col., Col., 175, 178

Mareth Line; 86, 88

Medjerda River, North Africa, 113

Miami Beach, Florida, 182

Midkiff, First Lieutenant, 68–69, 71

Miller, Robert P., Lt. Col., 31, 67, 80, 87, 95, 103, 105–7, 109–10, 112–13, 115, 117–18, 138, 145

Montequilla, Italy, 144, 147, 149

Montgomery, Bernard L., Gen., British army, 30, 70, 86, 88, 107

Mount Pantano, Italy, 144–45, 147–49, 151

Mount Vesuvius, Italy, 161

Mousetrap valley, North Africa, 113–14, 118

Muir, William E., 1st Lt., 2, 51, 58

Myers, Second Lieutenant, 67

Nelson, First Lieutenant, 67

O'Daniel, John W. (Iron Mike), Col., 28

O'Farrell, Rufus B., 68, 96

Omagh, Northern Ireland, 17–19, 21, 30

O'MoHundro, Wiley, H., Col., 162–63

Ondecker, First Lieutenant, 26

Openshaw, Frank, 1st Lt., 26, 68–69, 71, 138

Operation TORCH, 40

Oran, North Africa, 40–41, 54, 65–66, 86, 116, 121–22, 126–27, 129

Pakenham, Sir Edward, Gen., British army, War of 1812, 100

Patton, George S., Jr., Maj. Gen., 41, 99, 104–5

Perry, Second Lieutenant, 26, 28, 68

Phelan, John J., Lt. Col., 168, 171, 173–74, 176–77

Philip II, King of Spain, 27

Pichon, North Africa, 73–74, 85

Pickett, George E., Gen., Civil War, 89

Plan Buffalo, 168

Port Aux Poules, North Africa, 121–22

Pratella, Italy, 139–40

Raft, George, 156

"Recessional," poem by Rudyard Kipling, 119–20

Richardson, First Lieutenant, 68, 89, 95

Rome, Italy, 168, 171–72

Rommel, Erwin, German army field marshal, 70, 86, 88, 104

Roosevelt, Franklin D., U.S. president, 39

Roosevelt, Theodore, Jr., Brig. Gen., 75

Rosignano, Italy, 177

Royal Military College, Sandhurst, England, 108

Ryder, Charles W., Maj. Gen., 41, 50, 104–5, 111, 165

St. Angelo, Italy, 139, 153–54, 157

St. Cloud, North Africa, 66

Sale, Second Lieutenant, 126

Salerno, Italy, 128–29

San Pietro, Italy, 155

Sbiba, North Africa, 81, 84

Sears, Lieutenant Commander, British navy, 43, 55

Sellers, Raymond W., Capt., 68

Sheffield, HMS, British cruiser, 33–35, 39, 42–43

Shinn, Robert V., Capt., Maj., 1, 138

Siats, Second Lieutenant, 2

Sidi-bel-Abbès, 70, 128

Sidi Nsir Station, North Africa, 101–2

Smith, William E., 1st Lt., 68

Snellman, William F., Capt., Maj., 32, 43, 58

Sorrento, Italy, 142

Spanish Armada, 27

Sparks, Floyd, Capt., 26

Sperrin Mountains, Northern Ireland, 32

Stacy, Maurice, 1st Lt., Capt., 68, 113, 156

Stillwater, Minnesota, 31

Stokes, Second Lieutenant, 134

Stowe, Harriet Beecher, 27

Suck, Gustave N., 1st Sgt., 126, 135

Svoboda, Albert, Lt., Col., 70, 109

Sweeting, Harry W., Lt. Col., Col., 157, 162, 165, 168, 174

Swenson, Edwin T., Lt. Col., 31–32, 35, 43, 46–47, 49, 55

Tabarka, North Africa, 101

Tangears, Viso, Capt., French navy, 50

Tellas, Private, 46–47

Tenes, North Africa, 124

Terminal Force, 34–35, 37, 42–43, 53–54, 56

Thaler, Paul F., Capt., 31, 52

The Infantry School, Fort Benning, Georgia, 105

Thirty-fourth Division, 1, 22, 41, 56, 59–60, 65, 69–70, 99–100, 104–5, 121–22, 126, 128, 138, 147, 156, 165–66, 169, 172, 179

Thompson, Sergeant, 2

Tiber River, Italy, 173

Toffey, Lt. Col., 163

Trawick, Emory J., Capt., 32

Trotter, Staff Sergeant, 189

Tucker, First Lieutenant, 68, 106

Tunis, North Africa, 57, 65, 117–18

Tunisia, North Africa, 61, 65, 69–70, 73, 104, 111, 117–18, 122, 124

Tyler, James E., Maj., 178

United States Military Academy, West Point, New York, 105

Velletri, Italy, 169

villa of the Deux, Frères, 62

Viterbo, Italy, 175

Volturno River, Italy, 131–32, 135–37, 139, 141, 145

von Arnim, General, German army, 104

von Ruden, Anthony, 2nd Lt., 68

Voss, Leo, 1st Lt., 31, 38, 188

Wainwright, General, 13

Walsh, Larry, 2nd Lt., 2

Ward, Robert W., Col., 74, 77, 87, 115–16, 138, 156

Williamston, North Carolina, 181

Windsor, Sergeant, Captain, 126, 177

Young, First Sergeant, 135, 148

Zimmerman, First Sergeant, 77